YOUNG AGAIN

Veterans recapture a moment of youth
through Ageless Aviation Dreams Foundation

DAVID FREEZE

Published by:
Walnut Creek Farm Publishing
China Grove, N.C. 28023

Designed by Andy Mooney

ISBN 978-0-692-03399-9

On the front cover: Stearman (tail number 371SD) was built in 1942. It was manufactured by Boeing in Wichita, Kansas. This aircraft was fully restored around 2009 and gave its first dream flight in August 2011. It is primarily used by AADF in the western states.
On the back cover: AADF Founder and President Darryl Fisher greets Angus L Emerson. Photo by Thomas Graning, The University of Mississippi.

FOREWORD

I consider it one of my luckiest days when one of our Sport Clips franchisees in California called me to excitedly tell me about a wonderful program his company was supporting, Ageless Aviation Dreams. Sport Clips had long been actively involved with the VFW and other veterans' organizations, but I had never heard of AAD until that day. The thought of World War II veterans having the opportunity to go up in a Stearman biplane put a smile on my face….and I soon learned that my smile was nothing compared to the smiles on the faces of those aged warriors when they buckled in, and when they returned from their flights!

Having been a pilot in the Air Force, I was immediately attracted to Ageless Aviation Dreams. Sport Clips is proud to be a primary sponsor of Darryl Fisher's wonderful program, which began when he and his father started giving rides in his grandfather's Stearman to residents of their former assisted living homes after they picked up the newly restored plane in Mississippi. Realizing the difference this simple gesture was making in the lives of these members of the Greatest Generation, Darryl established the Ageless Aviation Dreams Foundation that eventually spread the joy of these flights across the country.

Starting with a single plane, the AAD "Air Force" now has three Stearman biplanes with two more coming soon. Over 2,000 flights to date, and Darryl's not slowing down! Our Sport Clips Team Members have been privileged to assist with many of these flights, and to a person they have all said that this was one of the most meaningful days of their lives. These young people have been great, helping with the participants and their families and cheering them on their great adventure. I don't know who enjoys these flights more — the selfless pilots who volunteer their time, the crew and helpers on the ground or the veterans themselves!

All of us owe these men and women a huge debt of gratitude, and being able to help bring a little joy to their lives is a privilege, a small way to say "thank you" for all that they have done for us. Working with Darryl and Ageless Aviation Dreams is a dream come true for not only those veterans who slip the surly bonds of earth to fly once again as many of them did decades ago, but for those of us who are fortunate enough to be part of this wonderful program. I am sure that you will enjoy reading about this program and the wonderful work Darryl and his volunteers are doing to brighten the days of those who deserve it the most.

— **Gordon Logan,**
Founder, Sport Clips

ACKNOWLEDGMENTS

As always, my heartfelt thanks go out to the people that I met along the way during my year of touring with the Ageless Aviation Dreams Foundation. I have spent many miles touring the United States of America by bicycle and then chronicling the journey. Touring by plane, especially on a small fleet of Stearmans, is quite similar. The people make the trip and once again, I have confirmed that fact.

The veterans and their families, many of whom you will meet shortly, were wonderfully willing to share their thoughts upon entering or exiting the plane. But even harder for many of them were the words that focused on their military exploits. I realized that I was being honored to hear the stories in the midst of honoring them with the dream flight. To all the veterans and their families, thank you for making this book possible and I hope you will enjoy reading it.

Thanks to Darryl Fisher who wanted to record a year in the life of his organization. I had a ball meeting everyone associated with providing the flights, including airport staff, those amazing caregivers at the various nursing homes and assisted living centers, sponsors and all the others who played a part.

Bill Fisher and all the AADF volunteers made for some enjoyable and memorable times and I felt at home with them as they went about their business. Many of them even contributed to the book, offering their own thoughts about why and how the magic happens.

Gordon Logan, founder and owner of Sport Clips, provided the foreword for an organization that he clearly believes in.

Chris Verner did his usual great work editing my words and creative director Andy Mooney made sure that the layout, graphics and much more were just as they should be. Merilyn Chaffee helped me with proper terminology, names and facts associated with the dream flights. She and Lynn Sommars provided the photos used within the book.

INTRODUCTION

A classic plane for classic Americans

Magic — The term most often used to simply recap a single day's experience with Ageless Aviation Dreams Foundation. At the end of a long day of flying honored veterans, crew volunteers look at each other and say, "I felt the magic today!" How do they describe the magic? You will find out when you read why they volunteer to take these veterans on "dream flights," a term coined by Darryl Fisher, founder and president of the organization.

But there is a good chance you will already know as you read how the Fisher family was consumed by flight, the doors that closed and opened so that Darryl Fisher could discover the magic and then experience a year in the life of this fantastic organization.

Along the way, you'll meet Mary Helen Foster, a 94-year-old former Women Airforce Service Pilot (WASP) who flew virtually every plane available before being honored with the Congressional Gold Medal. Then there was Dom Errichiello, who went ashore in one of the early waves at

Omaha Beach, climbed the cliffs to take out pillboxes on the way to being captured by the Germans and surviving an incredible escape.

You won't forget Ray Smith, who signed up to fly fighters but was then transferred to gliders in time to land 15 soldiers successfully behind the German lines at Normandy. Smith flew a Stearman in the Navy and the Army, just one of many WWII veterans already familiar with AADF's signature fleet of planes. Or B-17 bomber gunner Lloyd Smith, who was captured by the Germans and eventually rescued by Patton after more than a year as a POW, and who was honored in Mississippi with the 2,000th flight provided by AADF.

You'll learn why a veteran was moved to say, "You took me to a place that I haven't been in years!" and why another veteran said, "I feel like a human being again!"

Remarkable is another key word often associated with the AADF dream flight experience. Anticipation, honor, celebration and family are just a few more.

Turn the pages and enjoy learning more about what made 2016 an amazing and unforgettable year, fulfilling the purpose and intent of AADF, all centered around those historic planes and the perfect peace of flight for those who have given so much.

NOTE TO READERS

All memories listed in the following pages came from recollections of the honored veterans and their families. Every effort has been made to provide accurate information throughout the book.

Also, the choice of the word flyer in reference to those veterans taken aloft came after careful consideration. Flier is more often used as the modern term but flyer seemed more appropriate when considering the age of the veterans and the classic Stearman planes.

CHAPTER 1

A financial crash of epic proportion;
How the dream flight idea was born

Ageless Aviation Dreams was conceived with the idea of giving back to some of the U.S. veterans who've given so much to preserve America's freedoms. Since its birth as a "wild idea" in Darryl Fisher's mind in 2011, AADF has provided thrilling rides in historic biplanes to more than 2,200 grateful veterans and other senior citizens, traveling to more than 35 states — and counting.

In the following pages, you'll learn more about this remarkable organization and some of the remarkable people it has touched.

The most remarkable, of course, are the veterans who take the flights — many of them now in their twilight years but still up for a rip-snorting adventure from which they often emerge rejuvenated and re-energized. There are also remarkable people working behind the scenes to make it all happen — volunteers who fly the planes, keep them in tip-top shape, arrange the schedules and ensure participants have an experience they'll never forget. And finally, there's the remarkable Fisher family, for whom AADF combines a multi-generational love affair with aviation with an equally strong dedication to enhancing the lives of senior citizens.

Through the hard work, dedication and contributions of many people, AADF has become an inspirational success story. It's a story made all the more remarkable when you consider that its birth in 2011 followed one of the darkest periods in founder Darryl Fisher's life, when his financial world came crashing down.

■ ■ ■

Darryl Fisher's parents, grandparents and other relatives had been successful in operating nursing home facilities. They needed to re-invest in more of the same for tax purposes. Darryl was president and one of three partners in Pinnacle Health Care. He made a decision on Labor Day 1999 that would forever change his life.

John Harder, President of Sun West Management, asked Darryl, "Would you consider buying in and working for me for 15 percent of Sun West?" Harder planned to retain 75 percent of the company while other investors still held the remaining 10 percent. At the time, Sun West had 20 retirement communities. Darryl's relatives bought in, joining him in the venture.

After agreeing to the partnership, Darryl became the chief operating officer of Sun West on January 1, 2000. The company's 20 communities were in three states.

Just seven years later in January of 2008, Sun West had 285 communities in 38 states. The company owned two Citation jets, one purchased in 2004 and the other in 2006. Harder became a securities broker in 2006 and owned Canyon Creek Financial, a broker/dealer eventually owning land and farms valued at $500 million. By 2008, there were 10,000 Sun West team members and 18,000 residents.

Darryl had personally guaranteed $1.7 billion dollars in debt. He was responsible for senior living operations among other things and was so busy in the office that he seldom had time to visit with Harder.

During late 2007, Merrill Lynch went down. Sun West had $300 million with them in non-performing debt. General Electric had financed $340 million in performing debt. GE eventually bought up all of the Merrill Lynch debt, leaving their total at $640 million. Darryl and Sun West were $2 billion in debt overall at that point.

Darryl said, "We stopped paying investors, our capital was trapped and lawsuits started to crank up. One investor started to put in $400 million, then backed out. Over a three-month period of time, everything crashed. GE demanded financial advisors and then a chief restructuring officer. We stopped making payments."

Over 100 lawsuits were filed against Darryl, happening almost daily at both home and at work. Some of the Sun West properties began filing bankruptcies. Darryl met with regulators in South Carolina, Texas, Tennessee and other states. Through it all, Darryl said, "We are going to provide service to the residents!"

Harder filed for bankruptcy, but a federal judge denied the request. Another federal judge authorized a limited receivership, a process when the authority over decisions is removed from the officers and directors of the company and given to a custodial person with responsibility to operate the business. This is normally done when a company or enterprise cannot meet its financial obligations. The United States Securities and Exchange Commission oversaw the process.

"This was the first time ever in the United States that there had been a receivership of this magnitude. I got a huge lesson in the power of a federal judge, realizing that the judge can actually make the law during the process. But because of the judge, the banks had to stop trying to foreclose," said Darryl. In this case, the jurist was Judge Michael Hogan.

By this time, 75-80 communities were in foreclosure. Darryl was allowed to stay with Sun West but Harder and the chief financial officer were let go. Darryl was responsible for daily operations but was under the close scrutiny of Mark Schmidt, hired by the chief restructuring officer to see if Darryl had the skills to run the company. Schmidt had thirty days to decide. The SEC, the federal judge and the CRO eventually gave Darryl a chance to rebuild his career by proper management of Sun West through the challenging next steps.

Darryl continued to divest by selling 146 communities. Investors could take an early out by recouping 60 cents on the dollar owed. Those who stayed until the end eventually got all of their money back. Sun West was formally put through a bankruptcy for the new buyers, finalized when the company was sold on August 5, 2010. In November, 2010, Darryl left as the last employee.

The federal judge barred anyone from suing Darryl for any portion of the liability. A suit from Sterling Bank for $4 million was denied by the judge and no one else ever attempted any other legal action against Darryl. Darryl's net worth in December of 2007 was $150 million and by December of 2010, he was essentially broke. Investment bankers had offered the large sum to Sun West in 2007 for Darryl's part of the company, but Harder wouldn't sell, saying, "It's just not enough money."

The government decided to learn from what happened to Sun West. Darryl was interviewed by the FBI, the IRS and the SEC, line item by line item from 2006 to 2008. He answered questions on every check written. Darryl revealed that back in 2005, he thought that Sun West needed experienced help and contacted a friend with that knowledge from a similar situation about joining the company. Harder wouldn't allow it.

By December 2010, Darryl was tired but happy. He said, "It is not about what you have but it's who you are. This will not define us. My friends are not wealthy. I couldn't care less about the house." Darryl lost a 13,000-square-foot house complete with 30 acres, his own motocross track and basketball court.

Darryl decided to start over but things didn't immediately work out. His parents got their money finally from Sun West and Bill Fisher, Darryl's dad, paid off a red Stearman biplane that had just completed restoration in Mississippi. Ageless Aviation Dreams was about to be born.

CHAPTER 2

How flight evolved in the Fisher family;
Memories from Bill Fisher

The Fisher family got its first interest in powered flight back in April 1913. William Fisher, Darryl's granddad, climbed up a cherry tree in Peru, Indiana, at the age of 10. Little William heard a noise far in the distance, an engine noise that got louder and seemed to get closer. First expecting to find the noise coming from a car heading his way on a nearby gravel road, William realized in amazement that the noise was coming from above him and almost immediately spotted his first airplane. William's gaze followed the plane until it was long out of sight, entranced with what he had just seen. William didn't know it then but something bigger than himself, something that three generations later was destined to be the beginning of Ageless Aviation Dreams Foundation, would eventually come from this first sighting of an airplane.

Fast forward to 1923. William was in his senior year of high school in Artesia, California, about three miles from what is now Knott's Berry Farm. A high school friend had a motorcycle for sale and William wanted to buy it. He rode it home from school and his dad saw it later that evening, curious as to what it was doing there. William said, "It belongs to my friend and he wants to sell it. I want to buy it." William's dad had survived an unpleasant experience with a motorcycle in his own younger days, having lost control on a gravel road. That experience was still memorable and influenced his opinion.

"You take that motorcycle right back to your friend!" William's dad said. "I would sooner see you fly." William knew better than to make a smart reply, but he quickly thought, "All right, old boy, that is just what I will do." With that, William's dad became an unsuspecting advocate for general aviation.

William gave flying a try during the summer of 1939. By that time, he was married and had a son, William Jr., or Bill, who had been born in 1936. William's first flying lesson took place at the Compton, California, airport. The airplane was a 50-horsepower Piper J-3 Cub. William did shallow precision turns and stalls with instructor W.C. "Bill" Gage. William soloed on October 8, 1939, after just eight hours of instruction. That training was spiced with a couple of aerobatic flights in a Fleet biplane with a five-cylinder radial engine. Then, on April 16, 1940, William successfully flew his private license test flight. Although the flight was never signed off in his log book, he received pilot certification #95410.

In the meantime, William's brothers Bob, Charles and Dick were all taking lessons. Bob earned his license just after William on September 20, 1940. Charles also earned his pilot's license and Dick soloed before both decided to give up flying.

Flying continued for William and Bob as they advanced from Piper Cubs to Porterfields and moved their airport base to Anaheim, California. At Anaheim, the Porterfield dealer rented his planes for $4 an hour with a dollar of that applied to the purchase price of a new Porterfield. Both Bob and William solicited their friends to pay for flights to increase their total dollars toward the purchase of a new Porterfield F-65.

On December 17, 1940, William and Bob picked up their new Porterfield in Kansas City and planned to fly cross-country to Anaheim. The trip home was an adventure that included temperatures of 0 degrees Fahrenheit while flying over Odessa, Texas. They had no heater and were hampered by headwinds and low visibility. They flew low, using roads for landmarks. Cars often saw the airplane overhead and sped up to leave them behind.

From Tucson to Gila Bend, Arizona, William and Bob had an extremely low ceiling and encountered five Army Air Force Wildcat pilots upon landing. The planes were grounded because of bad weather, and the Air Force fliers were impatient to continue their flight eastward. One of the pilots ran over to William and Bob, asking, "Where did you guys come from?" He was told that they had flown the railroad from Tucson. Immediately, the Wildcat pilots warmed up their planes and took off for Tucson, following the railroad at an extremely low level.

After 14 stops and 11 hours and 14 minutes flying time, plus overnight stays in Odessa, Texas, and Tucson, William and Bob arrived in Anaheim on December 19. The pair continued building up their flight hours until October 12, 1941, when William moved his family to Washtucna, Washington, and leased the family wheat farm from his father-in-law. Less than two months later, the attack on Pearl Harbor and the declaration of war by President Franklin D. Roosevelt on December 7, 1941, ended private flying on the west coast and the Porterfield was sold.

Even though the flying bug had bitten the Fisher family pretty hard, William took two years away from flying due to the war and learned the farming trade. Bob applied for an instructor's position with the Army Air Force in 1942 but his blood pressure was slightly too high for military acceptance. He then applied at the Ryan Company, which had a contract with the Army Air Force to furnish civilian flight instructors to the military. Ryan Company physicals were not quite as restrictive and Bob passed his commercial check ride in a PT-22 on February 4, 1943. The next day, he passed his instructor's check ride for the Military Civilian Instructor program, again in a PT-22.

Four days later, Bob gave his first day of instruction. He

instructed at Ryan Field in Hemet, California, until he was released on December 18, 1944, and by early 1945, he was working on the family farm. During his employment, Bob logged 1,098 hours and 22 minutes of primary training. Bob learned to favor the PT family of Stearmans over any other military primary trainer. This was the dramatic birth of the Fisher family's Stearman love affair.

William had resumed his flying in December 1943 and rented several types of small private planes before buying a Piper J-3. A little over a year later, in January 1945, he joined two other wheat farmers for the purchase of a Waco UPF-7 biplane.

William began learning aerobatics in earnest, building a runway that started in his driveway along with a T-hangar. He sold the J-3 and when the farmers' partnership sold the Waco, William was left with no airplane. On December 5, 1945, he bought a 3-place Cub Piper J-5 but then sold it in June 1946. William, with Bob's help, began to pursue the purchase of a Stearman. He finally located one at the Beaverton airport, just outside of Portland, Oregon. That airport, like so many other historic small airports, was later turned into a town center mall.

This particular Stearman, serial number N49295, was all silver. On a cloudy day in August 1946, William and Bob flew it to the farm after "scud running"— or dropping their altitude beneath cloud cover — along the Columbia River from Cascade Locks, Oregon to Pasco, Washington. William and Bob had each purchased LK-10 WWII training gliders from Art Whitaker. Whitaker worked out of the old Portland, Oregon, airport alongside the Willamette River.

During its military service, the Stearman's Jacob engine had been removed and replaced with a Continental 220. Besides being used for aerobatics, the plane also doubled to tow gliders. Young Bill Fisher, William's son, entered the family story at that time as just the right size to hold the wing up during takeoff for the gliders and to retrieve 300 feet of nylon rope after the tow was over. Bill became skilled at doing both but eventually found ways to entice others to do the work while he rode in either the Stearman or the glider. Bill grew to love the family Stearman.

Sadly, on March 22, 1948, two days after Bill's 12th birthday, William sold the Stearman to a Wanatchee crop spraying firm that converted it to a spray plane complete with a R-985 Pratt and Whitney engine, a 1,600-pound capacity tank, metalized fuselage and a canopy-covered cockpit. As Bill watched it fly away from the farm, he promised himself to someday own another Stearman. Little did he realize that the day would be over 34 years later. Bill and his brothers kept track of that Stearman all through the years as it was used around the wheat country of eastern Washington State, where they lived. It was painful to see it sitting out in the weather and deteriorating from hard usage.

On October 14, 1982, Bill became the proud, but rather nervous owner of a Stearman, N58986, formerly owned by

Meek Dusters. In the summer of 1982, Bill's son Darryl's interest in restoring his Pontiac GTO Judge 400 Ram Air was replaced by his newfound interest in flying. He decided late one Thursday evening that he wanted to learn to fly. Bill said, "Darryl never does anything halfway! He took lessons and got his physical exam from his best friend's dad on Friday, didn't fly Saturday, but then flew Sunday and soloed on Monday." On the first weekend in August, 1982, the West Coast Stearman owners held a fly-in at Creswell, Oregon, 60 miles north of the Fishers' home in Roseburg. Darryl got up Sunday morning and started pestering Bill to drive them up to Creswell to see the Stearmans.

The day was rainy with clouds below the hilltops and Bill tried to talk Darryl out of it, but eventually he gave in. They arrived at the Creswell Airport to find five Stearman planes tied down and grounded because of the unusually low cloud ceiling. The pilots were all in the airport office shooting the breeze and hoping for a break in the weather. Bill and Darryl slipped in quietly and listened to their stories and comments.

Eventually, the biggest and tallest pilot acknowledged them and introduced himself as Doug Lusher. The Fishers told Lusher about William owning a Stearman at one time and about their love for them. Right away, Lusher said, "I've got a Stearman for sale for $10,000. I just dropped the price from $14,000." It was a retired spray plane and Bill knew something about those planes that had sprayed the family crops. He knew well the chemical smell that lingered in the cockpit of most spray planes.

Lusher gave Bill his business card and he also let Darryl ride across the airport to the gas pump in his beautiful custom Stearman. Darryl was ecstatic and on the drive home, he tried to persuade his father to go to Evergreen Airport in Vancouver, Washington, to look at the Stearman for sale. Bill held his ground, and clearly stated that he did not want to spend any time looking at a giant canister full of chemical smell. Darryl didn't let up and reminded Bill that he had a business convention in Portland in September, so why not at least call Doug in order to go see the plane.

Bill's convention was three days long and the first day was quite boring, so he gave Lusher a call. He wasn't at home but Lusher's wife invited Bill and his wife, Darlene, to come see the restored Stearman. The plane was so beautiful that even Darlene got excited about seeing the one for sale. Mary Jane Lusher was a commercial pilot herself and she seemed to know just how to approach Darlene, a strictly fair weather passenger. They all walked into the hangar and Bill climbed up on the wing walk and stuck his head down in the cockpit, but he detected no chemical smell at all. He decided that the metal fuselage covering was held on by Dzeus fasteners, and it could easily be removed for cleaning.

The Stearman N58986 was an old, beat-up spray plane that was white with orange numbers and the words "Meek Dusters" painted on the front of the fuselage. It had a silver rudder, an unpainted aluminum side cover, a ground adjustable propeller, Elmer's square tipped agricultural wings and a metal covered fuselage, complete with spray equipment. Darlene Fisher fell in love with the plane and felt that a second mortgage on their home was the proper way to handle the financial end of the purchase. Needless to say, Darryl was in total agreement.

Bill stayed at the Evergreen Airport that afternoon and took 2.3 hours of dual training with Wally Olson in his UPF-7 Waco. He came back the next day, did another hour of dual, then soloed for 1.2 hours. Previously, Bill had several hours in a Cessna 180 and most of his flying had been in tail draggers. He read the Stearman flying handbook thoroughly and spent several hours listening to Bob Fisher counsel him on flying Stearmans. This approach was probably not the best way to prepare to fly a 450 Stearman, but it worked.

By the summer of 1983, Darryl had gotten his pilot's license and returned home from college. He was able to solo the Stearman after duplicating Bill's training with Wally Olson. Then Bill found that the Wenatchee Spraying firm, now owned by the son-in-law of the man who bought William Fisher's Stearman, was selling out their Stearman stock and getting newer spray planes. Bill flew there and had the firm remove his Elmer's Agricultural wings and replaced them with a set of stock airfoil wings. He also bought a Hamilton-Standard prop hub with 2-30 blades.

At the same time, Bill's brother Tom, who had become a spray pilot himself, went to Wenatchee and purchased back Stearman N49295, Bill's dad's original Stearman. Their other brother, David, traded his Super Cub for Stearman N53113, another of the Wenatchee fleet.

In March 1984, Bill flew to Rio Vista, California, and helped Bill Decker take out the spray tank and install a seat in the front cockpit, along with a stick, rudder, brakes and safety harness. The back of the spray tank was the instrument panel for the rear cockpit so Decker replaced it and returned the instruments to the stock panel.

William and Darryl Fisher both joined Bill in Rio Vista to help remove the spray equipment. While there, William contracted with Decker to build him a stock blue and yellow Stearman which was delivered in 1985 in time for the Cottage Grove, Oregon, Fly-In during the first week of August. The Creswell, Oregon, Fly-In location was changed to Cottage Grove and has been there ever since.

Bill also purchased another Wentachee Stearman, N58501, in 1986 from a farmer friend who decided that the didn't want to use it to spray his own fields. In just under four years, the Fisher family had become a five-Stearman family, with three generations of current Stearman pilots. In 1987, Bill flew with William in his new Stearman, N585WD, on the right wing of the lead Stearman in the 50th Anniversary formation flight around the Golden Gate Bridge. William, at age 74, was the oldest pilot there.

Good things don't last forever and William lost his flight physical shortly thereafter and sold his plane.

William's first Stearman, N49295, bought back by Tom in June 1983, was in bad shape and starlings had gotten in through a hole in the upper wing fabric and made a nest. Tom took it apart and stored it in the Fisher hangar. David's Stearman was also taken apart and stored, as well as the one that Bill bought from a neighbor. Bill later gave this Stearman to Darryl. Bill kept the Stearman that he purchased from Doug Lusher patched up and flying until the mid-1990s, when it was retired to the Fisher hangar.

In 2004, Darryl bought William's first Stearman from Tom and a year later at the National Stearman Fly-In of 2005, Darryl and Bill met with Pete Jones of Air Repair. Everyone agreed to have him restore all three Stearmans, N49925, N58501 and N58986. Jones' generosity, skill and commitment to restoring Stearmans played a key role in the success of Ageless Aviation Dreams Foundation.

After returning from the fly-in, Bill and his son Bill Jr. stripped all the wings and fuselages and collected all the good parts along with a collection of spare parts, engines and other pieces that had accumulated during the process of trying to restore the Stearmans themselves. Everything was packed into two Roadway trailers and shipped to Air Repair in Cleveland, Mississippi, for restoration.

William's Stearman was finished first. Even though it was silver when he originally purchased it, the family wanted it painted blue and yellow to represent both of the Stearmans that William had owned, matching the structure of the first and the color of the second. This plane was delivered in 2008.

The plane that Bill had given Darryl was delivered in 2009. Bill's was also ready in 2009, but he had suffered unexpected financial difficulties during the recession of 2008-2010. Bill was unable to pay the final bill on the plane's restoration. He told Pete Jones to sell the plane to recoup the remaining restoration costs. Instead, Jones borrowed the money to pay himself and insisted on holding the plane for Bill. Finally, in March 2011, Bill was able to pay Jones what he owed but would always remember the exceptional way that he was treated. Thanks to Jones, the trip back home to Oregon in Bill's Stearman was possible, and with it came the beginning of Ageless Aviation Dreams Foundation.

AADF's mission actually began on March 28, 2011. Darryl and Bill were eating lunch at the Dallas airport between flights. Darryl looked at Bill and said, "Dad, I have a wild idea I would like to pursue. I want to know if you would be willing to let me use your Stearman to try it out on the way home."

Both men were on the way to Cleveland, Mississippi, to pick up Bill's completely restored custom Stearman, the Meek Dusters plane, which Bill had owned for 27 years. He had flown it and worked at restoring it during the first 24 years of ownership. The restoration was coming along slowly and Bill decided to contact Pete Jones at Air Repair for what became their 140th Stearman rebuild project. The plane was now literally new from spinner to rudder, including a Serve-Aero inverted fuel system. Bill was immediately concerned about using his beautiful Stearman for some "wild idea."

Darryl went on quickly to explain, "I would like to give a few World War II veterans rides on our way back to Oregon. I have a plan to call it Ageless Aviation Dreams. If you are willing to let me use your airplane, I want to take them for free."

Bill readily agreed to Darryl's idea. He said, "I am old enough to remember World War II very well and have only the highest regard for the military personnel and their families that gave so much during that conflict. Darryl and I have a close relationship and I was not surprised to find out that he had accurately anticipated my answer in advance and already had two rides lined up. One was in Oxford, Mississippi, and the other was in Jasper, Alabama."

The Fishers flew their Stearman from Cleveland to Oxford on March 29, 2011, with plans for giving that first "Dream Flight." The short 45-minute flight to Oxford was completed as they anticipated meeting military veteran Hugh Newton, a resident of a local assisted living facility. Administrator Sandra Enfinger brought Mr. Newton and his wife out for the flight. Bill said, "He loved the flight and we were exhilarated by his enjoyment." A few pictures and goodbyes preceded the flight to Jasper that afternoon.

In Jasper, Bill and Darryl were met by Carthell and Anita Williams from the local assisted lived facility. They drove the Fishers to a motel where they would spend the night. The next morning, the Fishers toured the facility and met Lloyd Latham, who was being honored with the second dream flight. Mr. Latham's family came to watch. His son was concerned about why the Fishers had offered the flight at all. Bill said, "He wanted to know why we were doing this, what our qualifications were, and continued to question us to make sure there was no cost or any other catch. The local newspaper reporters were there as well, photographing the flight and asking questions, almost as if we were trying to put some scam over on them."

Everything changed after the flight.

"The happiness of Lloyd and his family made us positive that Darryl had happened onto something really inspiring, something magical in fact, and we knew that we wanted to continue," Bill said. "The reporter was also convinced and gave us excellent local publicity."

The Fishers said their good-byes and loaded their small amount of baggage into the plane. They took off for Florida for the Sun and Fun Fly-In at Lakeland. The weather was overcast and the ceiling began to lower until they were flying at communication tower height in unfamiliar territory. With no weather improvement expected, Darryl executed a 180-degree turn and they hurried back to Jasper to wait for the weather to clear up.

It was in Jasper that the Fishers enjoyed a good visit with "Gordo" Sanders of Reno, Nevada, AT-6 racing fame who also ran the fixed base operation (FBO) providing services at the local airport. By returning to safety, they evaded a terrible storm that damaged many planes at the Sun and Fun Fly-In. Two days later the weather cleared and the Fishers flew to South Carolina for the weekend and then proceeded to give veterans rides in Georgia and at stops on the way home via San Diego and on up to Bill's home in Salem, Oregon.

The last stop before Salem was in Roseburg, Oregon, where they met Paul Bodenhamer Jr. who brought his father out for a dream flight. Paul Sr. was a B-17 pilot in World War II and had trained in Stearmans. They were so excited about what the Fishers were doing that Paul Jr. decided to volunteer his time and went on many trips later as helper, coordinator and publicity man. He donated his time and his company's expertise to design logos for the airplane, baseball hats to give to the veterans after the flights and T-shirts for the helpers and crews. Paul's help was invaluable as he assisted Darryl with establishing the Ageless Aviation Dreams program.

Word soon traveled and people from several states were beginning to request dream flights. It became obvious that the Fishers didn't have the resources to develop the program by themselves and would need to enlist the help of others to continue offering dream flights to military veterans.

Darryl had two Stearmans of his own, William's stock 220-Continental blue and yellow trainer, and a now renumbered custom 450, a sister ship to Bill's. This plane was white with a black checkerboard cowling and rudder. Darryl wanted to use these two and Bill's plane in the program. His wife Carol suggested that he create a 501(c)(3) nonprofit organization so he could receive donations to support the growing interest in AADF. Ageless Aviation Dreams Foundation soon became official. Darryl began to solicit donors while continuing to offer as many dream flights to veterans as he could.

Direct Supply Company of Milwaukee, Wisconsin, wrote the first contribution check to AADF and has continued its support every year since. Sport Clips is a major supporter of AADF, both financially and by providing volunteers who attend the Dream Flight events at the airports where they have nearby businesses. They also assist veterans in and out of the planes, often bringing snacks, soft drinks and other amenities for them.

The AADF crew is a special group of volunteers. Everyone donates their time to provide rides. Wayne Cartwright, a professional pilot who had AT-6 racing experience at Reno, was the first pilot to donate his time to the organization. Wayne was an exceptional person who loved the veterans.

The current listing of primary volunteers will follow later

in the book, with short biographies and special thoughts from each one. There is no payroll for AADF and all proceeds are invested back into the foundation to maintain the planes, pay for fuel, insurance and other operating costs.

AADF's mission to "Give Back to Those Who Have Given" has been the driving force behind the foundation's growth. The request for dream flights has increased substantially each year and it has become challenging to handle requests using just three planes.

To serve the growing number of senior military veterans, AADF is currently raising funds to purchase additional Stearman biplanes. Tim and Grace Newton of San Antonio, Texas, are raising money to purchase a plane to service that area. Tim is a 26-year U.S. Air Force veteran, having spent all of that time flying or training other pilots to fly.

In Stevens Point, Wisconsin, Marcia McDonald is spearheading an effort to purchase a Stearman for that area. The plane will eventually be called the "Spirit of Wisconsin."

Airport operators across the country have helped with the AADF mission by providing hangar space, allowing veterans to use their facilities and providing ancillary help of all kinds. Hundreds of businesses and volunteers have supported AADF, along with many local fire departments who have provided personnel with the knowledge to help those who are severely disabled and need to be carried in and out of the planes.

The family of Stearmans continues to fly and bring happiness to thousands of people, well past the original purpose of training men for war. On Memorial Day 2015 in Memphis, Tennessee, AADF gave its 1,000th dream flight. In October 2016, Darryl piloted AADF's 2,000th dream flight in Oxford, Mississippi — the same city where it all began.

CHAPTER 3

Darryl Fisher's memories of his early years

Darryl Fisher comes from a long line of flyers. William L. Fisher, Darryl's grandfather, took his first flight in California in 1939. William had bought an Indian motorcycle, a purchase his dad was not happy with. William Edgar Fisher (Darryl's great-granddad) said, "That thing is a deathtrap. You take it back. I would rather have you fly than ride a motorcycle!"

William Lavone Fisher bought his first plane in 1940, a LP-65 Porterfield. Darryl has since looked for the same exact plane but has not been able to find it. The Porterfield was a hit with both William and his brother Bob, who also started flying. While William Fisher flew only for personal reasons, Bob Fisher became proficient enough to train pilots for World War II.

The family encouraged William Fisher to buy a Stearman, the most popular pilot trainer during World War II. They found a Stearman in Beaverton, Oregon. and William bought it for $1,500. William and his wife, Dorothy, built a landing strip on their wheat farm in Washtucna, Washington. Darryl said, "My dad's first Stearman ride had come years earlier in that airplane, N49295, when he was about 11."

The Fishers kept that first Stearman for about three years, selling it in 1948 to a crop duster outfit. William Fisher was ready for another plane, the first of about 20 owned in his lifetime. Dorothy Fisher got a rare opportunity for free pilot training when her husband bought a new Piper Tri-Pacer. Included with the purchase was complete pilot training. In 1958, Dorothy got her pilot's license in Walla Walla. She eventually flew about 150 total hours but never piloted one of the family's Stearmans.

One of Darryl's grandmother's flight instructors played a unique part in continuing the Fisher family flying tradition. Boyd Hoops, 35 years later, also gave Darryl every check ride as a private pilot, commercial pilot, instrument rating and his flight instructor rating.

William L. and Dorothy Fisher had six kids whom they raised on their 1,800-acre farm. Darryl's dad, Bill, was the oldest. That farm became Darryl and his brother Bill's summer residence. Darryl said, "We learned to drive at seven years old. Both of us were tall and we could drive the loaded wheat trucks back to the farm where my grandmother would deliver them to the elevator." Darryl became very close to his grandparents.

The grandparents also considered venturing into Alaskan commercial fishing and then the nursing home business. They weighed both and chose the option that would do more for their community. After purchasing their first nursing home in 1965, they quickly bought two more, all of them in Oregon. While the Fishers still lived in Washington, they leased the Oregon nursing homes.

William George Edgar Fisher (Bill), Darryl's dad, graduated in 1965 from college with a degree in Greek and Hebrew. He taught history at Upper Columbia Academy near Spokane, Washington, until needed by his parents to run one of the nursing homes. William Lavone Fisher said, "You are honest and hard-working, I need you to take over one of the homes." Bill Fisher got his nursing home license in 1970 and did well enough to purchase two more nursing homes of his own. Eventually, Darryl's parents and grandparents became partners.

Active in the business until 1976, Bill had his wife serve as activity director while both boys worked in the nursing home as well. After 1976, all of that stopped when the homes were leased to others. Bill had no day-to-day job and neither did the rest of his immediate family. The summertime trips to the grandparents' farm also had ended.

The boys and Bill Fisher then became partners in William Fisher and Sons Construction Company. Darryl, then 13, and Bill, then 15, worked three summers and any other available time. Meanwhile, Darryl seldom thought about flying. He said, "I was agnostic to it. We liked motorcycles.

I was crazy about motorcycles and cars."

In the late '70s and '80s, the ultralight phenomenon had taken hold. Darryl said, "Flying an ultralight seemed really cool and it required no license. They caught my attention. My grandfather did his research and bought one in the winter of 1982. He flew it at the farm in Washington."

Grandfather William Fisher told Darryl that he could fly the ultralight after meeting one big condition. The elder Fisher said, "I will let you fly it, but it is like an airplane. It can kill you. You have to solo in an airplane first." With that, Darryl left the farm determined to quickly solo. In just four days, he had accomplished what usually takes much longer. Darryl said, "It was not smart, but I was motivated."

Arriving back at the farm, Darryl was ready to fly the ultralight. Grandfather William said, "You have to solo first." To which Darryl replied, "I did." He flew it only once in that summer of 1982, and never again. Darryl did take more powered flight lessons and began to enjoy it.

Darryl headed to Walla Walla University as a freshman in engineering. He said, "I hated it. Especially calculus and chemistry. I soon was struggling and dropped a few classes. I began to work at a gas station." Darryl's best friend joined him on a visit to the university aviation department and both were immediately interested. Darryl drove home to Roseburg and told his parents, "Me and engineering just aren't working out. Here is what it would take to change my major." Both parents agreed to the change for spring quarter of 1983 and by June, Darryl had his pilot's license.

Summer was filled with working at the airport, giving flight lessons or anything else needed. June of 1984 saw Darryl get his instrument, commercial flight instructor and multi-engine ratings. An internship with Adventist Health Systems in Florida and Texas provided some time to fly in the right (co-pilot's) seat for more experience. "I loved flying," Darryl said, "but being a professional pilot was not my ultimate goal. I was seeing the country but as a corporate pilot, I learned that I didn't like to wait. That is what corporate pilots do, they wait so someone else doesn't have to."

Now armed with a two-year aviation degree, Darryl went back to school to complete a four-year business degree in 1987. Along the way toward that degree, Darryl worked for Woodcutters Manufacturing as a pilot, which helped to fund his schooling. Though labeled as working in research and development, he never did any R&D. Cleaning bathrooms was still required but everyone liked Darryl because of his consistent work ethic.

Next was a three-month stint in human resources where Darryl often had to witness male employees providing urine samples for required drug tests. Not surprisingly, he hated the HR work. Then, at age 22, Darryl became shipping manager in this very cyclical business. Busy season was April through December for the porcelain stove manufacturer. Asked by the company president to manage the production facility, Darryl oversaw building 400 stoves.

With the increasing emphasis on emissions and air quality, the future didn't look quite so bright at Woodcutters Manufacturing. Darryl said, "I graduated from college with the business degree and didn't go back. But because of my work there, my only debt was a $2,500 student loan. My parents and grandparents still had two nursing homes leased, though one of them had an unusual back end agreement. That particular home would come back to the family for active operation in 1991. It was decided that I would eventually run that home." Darryl's uncle and aunt ran the other one.

A requirement was the six-month course called "Administrator in Training" specifically licensing Darryl to run a nursing home and fostering his role as a coach, mentor and leader. Darryl's uncle, Merlin Hart, taught him the course but federal and state exams were also required. Darryl passed the state exam but failed the federal one. In the meantime, he and Hart had started a medical supply company.

In August 1988, Darryl married Carol, whom he had met in a college Spanish class. It was Darryl's last class before graduation and he was the only male in the class. The other girls in the class pushed Carol to ask Darryl for a date and the rest is history. During October and November, Darryl did very little besides applying for new jobs at Carol's urging. He did get a job driving a school bus which allowed plenty of time for other things in the middle of the day. The wage was hardly lucrative although Darryl did enjoy the work. After quitting, he was surprised to receive a check for 45 days' work that totaled $3.50 once training expenses were taken out. Darryl said, "I wondered if Carol thought that she had married a bum."

Darryl did pass the federal licensing test on his second attempt and then knew that it was time to get a real job. After sending out numerous applications, Darryl was hired by Prestige Care in 1989 as a nursing home administrator. The CEO and majority owner was an accomplished pilot so most of the interview was about flying. Darryl took the required personality test and passed. He soon began flying the owner's twin-engine plane. Prestige eventually asked him to leave the first home and go to another one.

Darryl's dad called in February 1991 and Darryl took over their own nursing home while also running three properties for Prestige. There was little flying between 1987 and 1991 but Prestige donated their plane for political trips to Governor Barbara Roberts of Oregon, allowing Darryl to get some flight time. In 1990, Carol Fisher was able to use some of the proceeds of her lucrative real estate business to buy a Piper Cub. Darryl and his dad bought a Beechcraft Bonanza.

The partnership between Bill Fisher and Darryl, father and son, was going very well. Darryl said, "Dad and I worked really well together. He was a great partner and had great programs." Bill Fisher soon became a state representative and then later a state senator.

Another chance to expand the family business came in 1993 when Merlin Hart called and said, "I have an opportunity to buy another nursing home up north." Hart, Darryl and another partner bought the property and Darryl left Prestige. In 1997, the three partners bought four more properties. Darryl became president of the company.

Another change of direction occurred in 1999 when Darryl decided to sell everything that he was involved in, now nine nursing homes and an assisted living facility. A planned deal fell apart and the result was that the three partners who had formed Pinnacle Health Care bought out all of the other family members in the original group.

Waves of major change and upheaval loomed ahead ultimately resulting in Darryl losing nearly everything he owned, the story told in Chapter 1.

CHAPTER 4

Author's early impressions;
San Antonio on to Houston — March 9-11, 2016

This was the author's first time traveling with Ageless Aviation Dreams Foundation. It will also be the only chapter written in the first person, largely because I am only an insignificant part of the story being told about this fantastic organization. Still, there were certain expectations when I was immersed in the day-to-day operations and I think you will enjoy my early impressions.

I had first met Darryl Fisher in the late spring of 2013 in Salisbury, North Carolina, near where I live and often work as a free-lance writer for our local newspaper, the Salisbury Post. One of my favorite places for stories is the local airport and a regular topic has been the amazing veterans. With those interests, I was in the perfect place when AADF came to offer rides to the veterans from Oak Park Retirement. My past work for the newspaper had included other topics about the residents at Oak Park, including sky diving and helicopter rides, believe it or not. Many of the same residents became known to me through these particular stories and I was especially interested to see how they would do in an open-air cockpit plane that was more than 70 years old.

The veterans and friends from Oak Park were anticipating a great day as some of their group would actually take dream flights while others were on hand to watch and support their friends. As I remember, it was a warm and pleasant day. The Oak Park group was seated under a tent, some of the flyers more than a little nervous with anticipation.

I knew a few of the flyers and asked them their thoughts before getting in the plane. Several had never been in a small plane, certainly nothing like the historic Stearman with an open cockpit. Darryl had met many of the flyers the night before during a special veterans gathering.

The morning of the flights certainly had plenty of energy. As always, Darryl was at ease as he told about AADF, the plane, the flights and generally described what to expect for the day. Apprehension for the flyers seemed to lessen as he spoke and ended with: "OK, who is our first flyer?" Shortly afterwards, the smiles began. For me, I was immediately taken with what appeared to be such a wonderful concept and great organization.

The flights continued all day. And Darryl has returned to Oak Park again for what is now four consecutive summers. Oak Park expects another return engagement during 2017. By then, this book will be published and more memories will have been made.

The following is a brief recap of my own initial tour with Ageless Aviation Dreams Foundation. Darryl and I had talked about doing the book over the winter and our schedules both worked out for the series of flight tours described in the book. My own excitement about being a ground-crew member as well as the author of this chronicle of the "year in the life" of AADF was on a high scale. It didn't take long for me to feel the "magic" as Darryl and the other volunteers often say.

Darryl and I both took commercial flights to San Antonio, where we arrived on a Wednesday to pick up the plane and head toward a series of pre-arranged dream flights. We hoped to take the plane which had been wintered in San Antonio and head east. But when we arrived, weather was an issue, with clouds and rain. Nothing better was expected for the next morning, but Darryl was hopeful for a break that would let us get underway toward our commitments. We spent the night with Grace Newton, wife of another crew member and future pilot for AADF, in San Antonio. Tim and Grace Newton were heading a fundraising effort to purchase another Stearman that would be housed in the San Antonio area.

Steady rain overnight continued into Thursday morning. The ceiling was low, with rainy and breezy conditions. We had breakfast at Stinson Field, built in 1915, where our Stearman waited. Our goal was to make it to Houston later that day, about 120 miles away. There were scheduled dream flights along the way. Everything was at the mercy of the weather, with severe flooding already reported in many parts of Texas due to the heavy rain.

Around midday Darryl thought he saw a hopeful weather window. We took off into a headwind with drizzle falling and a ceiling of 1,000 feet, plenty for the Stearman. As we headed east, that ceiling lowered gradually to the point that Darryl and I talked about watching for towers. Even with the less than perfect conditions, I loved the flying time. Below us, we could see areas of severe flooding, and ahead any bright spots in the sky had begun to disappear. With the ceiling now below 400 feet, Darryl decided to return to San Antonio and try again the next morning.

The flight back was a little quicker with the wind behind us. The ceiling remained low but we landed safely. A second attempt the next morning looked better from the start with some higher skies, but gradually we encountered yet another storm front, causing us to land and wait for an hour at a small rural self-serve airport. Darryl figured out how to get inside the building to wait out the weather. With just minutes to spare after refueling, we were off again in hopes of the first dream flights of the tour.

We landed in Friendswood, Texas, under improving, yet breezy conditions. With just a few hours available for the dreams flights, Darryl quickly went to work. He told me that this smaller type of airport with little air traffic was the kind that he preferred.

The first flyer was Mary O'Neill, 88-year-old wife of deceased Air Force veteran John O'Neill. She had met her husband while he was in the service at Madison, Wisconsin. He was a rocketry officer and loved flying. Mary said, "He kept in touch with lots of the Korean War pilots after his service from 1951-1956. These days, I don't have a lot to look forward to, but I am certainly excited about this flight."

Leslie Harris was proud of his service in the Navy from 1944-1946. He was in a carrier aircraft service unit, mostly working with the TBM-3E bomber/torpedo planes. These planes had a pilot, gunner and bombardier. Harris' responsibility was to service the planes, gas them up and park them.

Another military wife was 81-year-old Juanita Schaefer. Her husband was a lieutenant colonel in the Air Force. He flew in Vietnam and was a member of the first all-jet training class. Service points included North Africa, Southeast Asia and several other foreign countries. This was Juanita's first time in an open cockpit plane and one of the few times that she had flown in a small plane. "My husband never flew the family for pleasure," Juanita said. "He always said it was his job to fly."

The last flyer of the afternoon was Christopher Reuter who served in the Navy from 1945-46. Reuter was responsible for driving a truck along the shorelines while protecting them from assault by water. Reuter served six months before the war ended and stayed in while others with more seniority were sent home.

Reuter's wife was a pilot with the Civil Air Patrol. He said, "I got to fly on planes with her. She was very good and took us through rolls and spins. My wife had an amazing ability to fly."

Darryl and I flew on to Houston that night, landing just before dark. It was the first time that I became aware of the presence of smells from the ground while in the plane. Lights were just coming on below us as we neared the end of the short hop to Houston and the Pearland Regional Airport.

The first flyer out of a group from Spring, Texas, was one that Darryl and I were both excited about. Mary Helen Foster was a Women Airforce Service Pilot (WASP) during World War II. She was listed as a civilian attached to the Air Force and was awarded the Congressional Gold Medal, one of the nation's highest civilian awards. Foster remembered that the Stearman was the first plane that she flew in a career as a test pilot that lasted from 1943 to 1960. She was 94 on the date of her dream flight.

A Marine stationed at Pearl Harbor during the Japanese attack of December 7th, 1941, Eugene Velten Bell was 93 as he prepared for his own dream flight. Bell remembered being ordered to a football field and told to use firearms to shoot at the Japanese planes. Reaching the rank of sergeant, he later used a 60-caliber machine gun in other areas in the South Pacific and lost two fingers while working on a machine. Bell helped with building bridges and roads.

Bell became a pilot after the war and used to rent planes for the fun of stalling them in a climb. He also once rented an amphibious plane, but it had been about 50 years since he had last flown before that day.

Fran Cheadle was a military wife who was married to an artilleryman during the Korean War. She had recently gone skydiving with her grandson at age 81 and planned to do it again in four years. Fran had 12 grandsons.

Another military widow, Barbara Kinard was married to a National Guard veteran. She had two grandsons in the Marines. Barbara was so excited that she didn't want to eat until after the flight.

The last flyer for the afternoon was Phil Rowe, a 92-year-old chief petty officer who served from 1941 to 1970. Rowe served on 10 different ships, usually transports, and was often responsible for munitions. He took the equivalent of two trips around the world. Rowe said, "My time in the service sure went by fast."

On hand in Houston was Spring Creek Village Marketing Director Cheryl Spell who handled escorting the flyers out to the plane, a lunch and ferrying residents back to the facility. She said, "What a great day for our residents. Thank you so much for bringing the plane and brightening their day!"

Also with us all day was Nancy Orozco of Sport Clips. Nancy spent the day helping the veterans and military wives by buckling them in the harness and securing their helmet correctly. Her attitude and bright personality added to the wonderful event. I have maintained contact with Nancy since that day of flying in Houston. She was married later in the year. Nancy actually dropped me off at the airport in Houston to complete my first AADF tour. Darryl also flew home commercially later the same evening after arranging for hangar storage of the Stearman.

CHAPTER 5

Dream Flights —
Atlanta, April 26-28, 2016

T wo days of dream flights were planned at the historic Dekalb Peachtree Airport in Atlanta, scheduled around a day of maintenance and some promotional marketing. Flights during this tour would be in the blue and yellow Stearman.

Darryl was excited to have so many World War II veterans coming for flights. Tuesday, April 26, dawned bright and beautiful, a perfect day for flying.

First flyer for the day was Ted Shimkus, 90 years old and originally from Connecticut. Shimkus enlisted in 1943 at the age of 17, straight out of high school. Originally sent to flight school, Shimkus eventually graduated from radio school at Scott Field, Illinois. Afterward he was based in the Azores.

One special memory for Shimkus was when he took the test to move to training as a B-17 bomber gunner. Rules stated that anyone over 6 feet was too tall and wouldn't qualify. Shimkus kept slouching until a lieutenant came over and made him stand up straight to his full height of 6 foot 2 inches. Shimkus said, "That officer saved my life. He washed us out of the B-17 program. Lots of those gunners didn't come back."

Shimkus continued, "I had some good memories from the war too. I once talked to Frank Sinatra and some of his showgirls. And I used to watch the P-51 Mustangs as they flew into Iceland. We saw some of those huge Russian transport planes too."

Postwar, Shimkus worked for 34 years with Sikorsky Aircraft. "I worked in manufacturing, engineering, tooling and purchasing," he said. "We also worked on the Black-hawk program and built the presidential helicopters. All this and I never flew in one." Shimkus, who attained the rank of sergeant in World War II, built his own house. His parents were both born in Lithuania and a daughter was a pilot herself.

After his dream flight, Shimkus was all smiles. He added, "I wanted to make my buddies jealous by doing this flight. I didn't want to do barrel rolls. It actually was a very easygo-ing flight. I thought it would be loud but it wasn't. The flight was fun!"

Bill Kirkpatrick was born in Spring Garden, Alabama, and later moved to Rome, Georgia. Serving in the U.S. Navy from 1947 to 1949, he joined another brother in the Navy and one in the Army. Kirkpatrick's time in the service was mostly spent on an AO-Tanker refueling ship before being transferred to an LST (a tank-landing ship), eventually making it to Guam. He also served on an LCVP, used for transporting troops or jeeps.

A special service memory for Kirkpatrick included an officer ordering him to proceed directly to the Officer's Club. Kirkpatrick quickly replied, "I am the captain of this ship. You can't order me where to go."

Remotely related to Elvis Presley, Kirkpatrick originally settled post-service in Los Angeles. He said, "I should have stayed there but made the bad decision to move to the North Georgia town of Rome. I have lots of questions to ask God about why I ended up in Rome."

Kirkpatrick enjoyed his dream flight and spent the time looking at the state of repair of the different roofs along the way. He used to be a roofing inspector and paid close attention to how the actual repair had been done.

An Air Force Academy graduate from 1963, Jeffrey Heal was a Vietnam vet. He suffered from multiple myeloma due to exposure to Agent Orange. Heal also volunteered at the Arbor Retirement Homes. Heal served almost twelve years, including two tours in Vietnam. He flew an A37B fighter bomber and then moved to KC-135 tankers. Heal said that at one time, he was the youngest double-rated officer in the Air Force after achieving ratings as a pilot and navigator.

Treatment for the cancer had continued for one and a half years. Heal said, "The VA is taking good care of me." Heal received his Air Force Academy diploma from President John F. Kennedy, after having marched in his inauguration and before seeing him again at Soldier Field in Chicago for an Air Force/Army football game.

Darryl allowed Heal to take the stick during the flight. Heal said, "I only wanted to fly the plane straight and level. Darryl wiggled the wings, which was the signal for me to take the stick. It was my first time ever in an open cockpit plane and my first flight in three or four years."

Often a person about to experience a dream flight can be a little apprehensive. Such was the case with Alex Eggers, 88 years old and a former paratrooper with the 82nd Airborne. Eggers served in the U.S. Army from 1945 to 1947, based at Fort Bragg in Fayetteville, North Carolina. His wife, Jean, and daughter, Kim Stasierowski, were on hand for the flight.

Eggers, from Pennsylvania and then Indiana, had known for about a month that he would fly on this day. He said, "I was definitely apprehensive. It was similar to my first parachute jump. Eventually jumping became much easier, just the same as the dream flight as it progressed." The Eggers family was all smiles and personality following the dream flight.

A lifetime Atlanta resident and mother of two sons, Lollie Sever enjoyed 56 years of marriage to Air Force veteran James Sever. Lollie said, "He served in Mississippi and in Korea but he didn't talk much about his duties. I am not sure of what he did."

Sever had never been in a small plane. While strapping in for the flight, she asked Darryl, "Does my helmet look as good as yours?"

Following her time aloft, Sever said, "The flight was wonderful, amazing!" She promptly kissed Darryl. "I am sorry I embarrassed him," she said. "This flight has been one of the highlights of my life!"

The final flyer of the day was someone who was no stranger to flying, but from a much different angle. Helen Chapman, age 94, was a control tower operator at Shaw Field in South Carolina. Chapman went along on training flights and did fly in a similar plane although she did not care to be a pilot. Chapman served in the Army Air Force from 1943 to 1945.

Accompanied on the day of the dream flight by her niece, Dorothy Drake, Chapman had worked in Washington, DC, at the Pentagon and at Patrick Air Force base as a contract employee. Drake said, "She also worked in the Philippines and in Thailand. The government wanted her services so badly that they flew her personal car to the Philippines, a fact that made her very popular with her co-workers."

Darryl Fisher had set aside Wednesday, April 27, for commitments other than flying. The day began with an oil change at the Priority Jet hanger. Mike Blitch of Auburn, Georgia, and Jordan Floyd of Athens, Georgia, provided tools and conversation while Darryl meticulously changed the oil. Blitch got a short sightseeing flight for his efforts, something that the Ageless Aviation pilots often do to maintain long-lasting relationships.

Next up was a marketing meeting with the local hospice organization across the runway at Epps Flying Services. Representatives of more than a dozen hospice locations eagerly listened as Darryl described how the Ageless Dreams organization had evolved.

Here was some of what Darryl told them. His dad, William Edgar Fisher, had bought a Stearman and needed it flown back to Oregon. He asked Darryl to fly the plane after they struck an agreement that would provide flights for elderly veterans at some of the gas stops.

Hugh Newton, a World War II veteran, got the first ever dream flight in Oxford, Mississippi. The second flight went to Lloyd Latham in Jasper, Alabama, another WWII veteran. Latham died a year later and had a picture from his flight on the casket. The Fishers knew that the WWII generation had changed the course of history and that the vast majority of pilots from that era had trained in the Stearman planes.

The Ageless Aviation Dreams Foundation gives dream flights to veterans and their widows during a season that lasts from late March until Veteran's Day in November. All organization members are volunteers and are paid in satisfaction only, to which Darryl often adds, "And with that, we are always overpaid."

The two oldest passengers so far to make a dream flight

have both been 102. The oldest veteran in the United States at 108 years of age declined to fly earlier this spring. Darryl said, "We want to give them a meaningful event at this special time in their lives. Each participant gets the hat ceremony and a flight certificate."

Since he was presenting to a hospice group, Darryl related a pertinent story. He said, "Once when we were in Cheyenne, Wyoming, a man in hospice care approached the plane using a walker and oxygen. But he quickly proceeded to unhook the oxygen tubes and was able to climb easily into the plane. He is still alive and is no longer in hospice care. When someone goes on the dream flight, magic happens!"

About 700-800 dream flights should happen during 2016 at about 20 minutes per flight. Darryl said, "It is not just a ride, but a dream flight experience, honoring the veterans' sacrifice for all of us. I always suggest that when the flight certificate and photos come in, have a ceremony for your veteran."

"Sometimes the veterans cannot help get themselves into the plane. The dream flight crew has training in the loading process and is making a continual assessment during that process. Ageless Aviation Dreams' core principles start with safety and they take every precaution mechanically. Communities shouldn't predetermine who can fly. All the flyer needs is some leg strength and yet almost every time, even those without significant leg strength have been assisted into the plane."

"Someday, someone will die in the plane," Darryl acknowledged. "Society is so afraid of any such adventure for the elderly, but our legal counsel advised us not to have the flyers sign a waiver. We get independent requests. One homebound guy and WWII veteran took a flight with us, perked up and had a night on the town with his daughter, then died ten days later. The power and awe of what we do makes me still get goose bumps."

No specific wealthy person is behind the Ageless Aviation Dream flights. Sport Clips, the largest donor, has never asked to put its name anywhere on the planes. Darryl added, "Without the donors, we won't fly. I tell the potential sponsors to write us a check if they believe in our mission. One donor stopped contributing because his logo was not on the plane. We didn't want them back. We do want businesses connected with the local culture, are family oriented and have some of the same goals. We have never sent out a donor letter."

After the presentation, those in the meeting were given a tour and photo opportunities with the plane and another question and answer session ensued. Many of the hospice locations asked how to get on the list for dream flights and Darryl graciously ran through the steps to make it happen. As the meeting broke up, Darryl told several of the attendees that he looked forward to seeing them soon.

Fred Hatterick was the first flyer of the next day. Fred

had his wife, Doris, by his side until he got in the plane. Having served for four years of active duty aboard a repair ship, Fred was especially apprehensive about taking his dream flight. He had never been in an open cockpit plane. Doris was worried for him as well, saying that Fred had medical issues and added, "I just hope he will be OK."

As Fred and Darryl flew away into the eastern sky, Doris stood waiting and watching with occasional tears in her eyes. She asked, "Which direction will they come back from?" Doris kept watching until the plane came into sight and safely landed.

Out of the plane and back on the ground, a different Fred began to speak. "This was very, very enjoyable. A real experience!" he said. "Something great for this late in life. I'm 85! I didn't think something like this would ever happen. I wasn't worried once we got up in the air. It is like I was in a dream, it was so comfortable."

Doris said, "What did you see? I have been so worried for him, but also excited for him. This was all so emotional for me. My heart is still pounding!"

As he hugged his wife, Fred said, "She was worth coming back to. Next to getting married, this was the most exciting thing I have done."

A four-year veteran of World War II as a U.S. Marine, John Gass III landed in the first wave assault on Iwo Jima. He was wounded in the first few days of the battle and evacuated. Other service took Gass across the Pacific twice and to Okinawa. He said, "I value the fact that I was able to survive such combat."

After the 92-year-old Gass finished his dream flight, he said, "It was not too breezy. I was very excited about the flight. This made for a very nice day for me. I only flew once in Hawaii."

Annie Veal, a 94-year-old Air Force veteran, classified herself as "just a paper pusher." She said, "I was born in Atlanta and served in Atlanta. I wanted to go overseas but didn't. I have been wanting to do this flight. My heart is beating, not because I am nervous, but because I am excited. This flight will be the best thing for the rest of my life."

Another WWII veteran was Morris Berg, who served in the Navy during 1944-45. His service was on a Liberty Ship in the mess hall. Berg said, "I wanted to see the world and I did. I was glad I made it back, but the Navy didn't disappoint me. It was something that had to be done and it was done."

Originally from Brooklyn, NY, and now 89 years old, Berg said after his flight, "I am one satisfied customer, no question about it. Everything looked beautiful. I have been on a plane but nothing like this."

Another flyer, 95-year-old Jim Armstrong, had been an Army Air Force pilot during his WWII service from 1942-45 and was very familiar with the Stearman. "I had flown the Stearman often," he said. "When we got a new plane, we did lots of cockpit time. The Stearman would do 80 miles per hour, but it has been years since I have been in a plane."

Originally from Pickens County in North Georgia, Armstrong hitchhiked to Atlanta to Fort McPherson to join the Army Air Force because he was worried about being drafted into the Army and being sent to the infantry.

CHAPTER 6

Dream Flights —
Salisbury, N.C., May 30, 2016

ADF made their fourth consecutive summer visit to Salisbury and Oak Park Retirement in 2016. Residents had come to expect Karen Leonard, activities director, to line up the flights and always planned to make a day of it. The day dawned sunny and warm as the residents waited under a tent next to the main terminal building to either go flying or cheer on their friends.

As usual, Darryl gathered all the residents before the first flight and described what to expect during the day. A few of the residents had questions but it was not long before the first passenger, Ron Hands, was ready to climb aboard the plane. Hands was an Army sergeant who served from 1950-58, part of it in Korea during the war. He only served there for 90 days, after which he came back and transferred to the National Guard. Both of Hands' parents were buried in Arlington National Cemetery after his dad retired as a full colonel.

An 85-year-old Air Force veteran, Ned Thomas served in

Korea from 1951-55. He served in a very cold mountainous area where the only way in was flying or walking. Thomas was so excited to fly and wanted to take pictures while aloft.

The first part of a married military veteran couple was Margaret Snelling. She served in the Women's Army Corp from 1952-55. At 86, Snelling said, "I was a corpsman, relieving men so that they could go to the battlefront." She finished basic training at Fort Lee near Petersburg, Virginia, then moved on to Texas and eventually to Heidelberg, Germany.

Snelling, originally from Mooresville, North Carolina, remembers giving electrocardiograms to generals and once forgot to put in the film. She thought she would be in trouble but was not. Snelling later served as the historian for the local DAV (Disabled American Veterans) chapter in Salisbury where she was part of the auxiliary.

Before her flight, Snelling said, "Two thumbs up now that I am strapped in. Do I have a stewardess? I love you, Herman!" After returning, she added, "Best landing I ever had. Do I have to get out?"

Mayor Karen Alexander of Salisbury greeted the Snellings as Margaret got out and Herman got ready to climb in. She told them, "Thank you for your service and I know how excited you must be to fly. I was a pilot myself. I can't think of another more special day than to be here with these veterans. These flights are bringing back their beautiful smiles."

Herman Snelling served in the Army from 1953-74 in an advisory position while ranked as a platoon sergeant. Originally from Belmont, N.C., he served in Alaska, Italy, Germany, Korea, Vietnam, Thailand, Laos and France, most of those in various support positions.

Herman met Margaret when both were at Johnson C. Smith University in Charlotte. She enlisted, then got married. Herman was drafted and also got married. Both marriages ended and Herman's mother told him that Margaret might be available. Herman went the next morning and found her and the result has been a 38-year marriage.

Originally from Oregon, Army veteran Bob Horand served during the Korean War from 1950-52. He stayed stateside and was responsible for assigning personnel. At 88, Horand told the crew that he had soloed a plane before, in 1949 and at his own expense, and was asked if he wanted some stick time. Horand replied, "Oh, no!" but added after the flight, "I thoroughly enjoyed the flight. We saw the Food Lion warehouse, the VA, downtown Salisbury. It was very smooth. This was an outstanding experience and just the perfect length."

Marine Corps veteran Tom Nolan served from 1969-73, including a tour in Vietnam. Nolan practiced law in Florida but had suffered three heart attacks, COPD, cancer and PTSD since being exposed to Agent Orange. "I have had just about every disease in the book," he said. "My dad had the most carrier landings in history through 1980." For Nolan, it was his first-ever flight in an open cockpit plane.

After enlisting in the Navy at age 17, Earl Graves Sr. served for 20 years that included WWII and the Korean War, mostly on destroyers. Some responsibilities included logistics for fuel, food and ammunition. Originally from Alaska, Graves, 87, was the pilot of the catapult plane on the ship. He was only launched one time, in search of submarines ahead of the ship as it was on the way into Pearl Harbor.

Sport Clips Area Manager Nikki Robey and Lexie Million passed out commemorative pins to the veteran attendees. Robey said, "Being here is so emotional. It won't be our last time. If we can help out these fine people, then we will."

Navy veteran Walter Leather served from 1943-46 during WWII. Most of his service was on destroyers after enlisting at age 17. Leather, 90, traveled to China, Korea, the Philippines, New Guinea, Okinawa and the Panama Canal. He also experienced two typhoons. Originally from Fall River, Massachusetts, Leather grew up next to the home of the infamous ax-murderer Lizzie Borden. He lost his wife of 65 years just five months prior to his dream flight.

The final scheduled flyer for the day was former Rowan County commissioner and Army veteran Hall Steele. Steele served from 1946, mostly in the military police around the Manhattan Project in Los Alamos and at Sandia Base, the principal nuclear weapons installation for the U.S. Department of Defense from 1946-1971.

Activities Director Leonard thanked the AADF crew before returning with her residents to Oak Park. "These are such special days," she said. "I look forward to planning next year as soon as we can. We have so many honored veterans that we just simply can't do enough for."

On a layover weekend in Salisbury, Darryl ran the local Bare Bones 5K race in one of his AADF shirts. He planned to do it again if possible for 2017.

CHAPTER 7

Milwaukee and Northbrook, then on to Stevens Point;
Bill Fisher joins crew — June 7-9, 2016

Expecting a very busy week, the AADF crew had visits planned to Milwaukee, Chicago/Northbrook and Stevens Point with the 1944 red and white Stearman taking the starring role. Darryl and Jared Jezensky were the pilot and ground crew but special assistance came from Darryl's dad, Bill Fisher. Bill Fisher owns this Stearman and had plenty of expertise to enhance the many conversations that happened during the week.

Milwaukee is the home of Direct Supply, a provider of various products and services to the Senior Living industry. Direct Supply wrote the first check in support of AADF.

Air Force veteran Robert Houck was the first flyer of the day on June 7th in Milwaukee. The 81-year-old Houck brought a special skill set to this tribute for veterans. Houck served near the end of the Korean War but was never a pilot during his service. Following his stint in the Air Force, Houck became a commercial pilot and eventually flew 1,500 hours on various large planes and also helicopters. As vice president of operations, he developed simulators for pilot training. He sold time on his simulators to other airlines.

Houck never owned his own plane but became a member of several flying clubs that had planes. He said, "My life wish is to fly a Stearman and I realize that most pilots aren't trained well on tail draggers. I appreciate that these volunteers have brought this plane here to take us on the dream flights."

Houck got his wish when Darryl let him fly the plane. Darryl said, "He did very well." Houck added, "There was less vibration than I expected and it handled nicely. I am probably going to donate to this organization."

The next dream flight recipient was Clarence Guenther, also known as Buddville or simply Bud. Guenther served in the Navy from 1943 to 1946 and the 92-year-old had World War II duties that included torpedoman, gunnery work on 20-millimeter cannons and some plane maintenance as seaman first class on an escort aircraft carrier.

Guenther was joined by his wife, Eileen, and daughter Lilly along with her husband, John. Guenther, then 92, joked, "They are all retired but I had to take a day off to be here."

Robert Muehlbaur came for his dream flight with his son John and wife, Betty Elizabeth. Muehlbaur, 93, had served in World War II from 1942 to 1945 as a U.S. Marine. His biggest engagement was at Majuro in the Marshall Islands and finished his service as a corporal.

Muehlbaur's wife, Betty Elizabeth, joked that when his military commitment was over, he went from one battle right into another. She was jokingly referring to their marriage, which had lasted 71 years. When Muehlbaur was asked if he was ready to fly, he said, "I am just ready to get it over with."

Darryl asked Meuhlbaur to take his cap off to prepare for the flight, and he was apparently concerned about getting it back. Darryl laughed and said, "Oh, you should see our hat collection."

Following the flight, however, his enjoyment was obvious. "It was an absolute privilege to fly with Darryl," he said. "It was very emotional for me." He remarked on the large bodies of water around Milwaukee and enjoyed seeing the roads, highways and little homes.

Flying next was Ed Aufderheide, a World War II Coast Guard seaman from 1944 and 1945 whose ship had ferried troops to England and Germany. He remembered that his best trip landed on the day that the war against Germany ended. There was already another happy load of troops ready to return to the United States. At 88, Aufderheide had never been in a plane.

The oldest veteran of the day was 96-year-old Clarence Harms, who had served in the Navy from 1944 to 1952. Harms served both on submarines and sub tenders and traveled all over the world. He was the first generation in his family to have American citizenship following their move from Germany. Harms was later employed with Boeing, Lockheed and with the Apollo space flights.

Another interesting participant was Jack Whitefield, a 92-year-old British native who served in the Royal Navy. Whitefield joined at 17½ years old and spent much of his service doing convoy work. Highlights included trips to Africa, India and Australia. His ship escorted the Queen Mary, the largest ocean liner of its time, when it was used for a troop carrier.

While at sea, Whitefield was a quartermaster who assisted in secondary steering. He said, "I served below decks on destroyers where the primary steering was done on the bridge. I was near the torpedoes. The Germans had vibration-seeking torpedoes and of course I was working nearest to the biggest vibration on our ship."

Once while on convoy duty, Whitefield's destroyer actually escorted his sister's ship but he didn't know it at the time. Her ship was headed to Burma. Both of Whitefield's brothers were killed while flying on British Lancaster bombers during the war. One brother was a tail gunner and the other was a navigator.

Whitefield said, "After World War II, I fell in love with a British girl and we went to Canada for 10 years. My sister-in-law was living in the U.S., so we came here. I have been looking forward to flying. At this price, I would fly anywhere!"

Another World War II veteran, Bob Nieman, was next

in line. Nieman, age 88, had served in the Navy as a boiler tender from 1944 to 1946, spending a year on a destroyer. He was called back to serve during the Korean War from September 1950 to March of 1952. Nieman said, "During Korea, I was a lead infantryman even though I was in the Navy. I had a lot of responsibility but was still a boiler tender first class. Earlier I spent some time in Japan at a repair base."

After his flight, Nieman, who is from nearby Madison, remarked, "Darryl told me to look at all my fans waiting for me. I told him that I must owe all of them money. Last year, I watched the dream flights, but I wanted to participate this year."

The long line of World War II veterans continued with Bob Loss, who served in the signal corps from 1943 to 1946 in the 13th Air Force. Loss was part of a 92-man unit that used radios and teletypes for communications and also provided maintenance for those systems. Loss said, "Our unit was formed for North Africa but we were sent to the South Pacific. We went to Guadalcanal about four months after the fighting and then on to Hawaii. I knew how to type and they made me a clerk. Everything was new to me. Most of it was fun and I was very fortunate."

Loss had basic training in St. Petersburg, Florida, where he was housed in a hotel. They drilled on the parking lot or the golf course, wherever space could be found. Loss suffered the death of his father and a bout of scarlet fever and tonsillitis while at Guadalcanal.

While rated as a private pilot, Loss had never flown a stick airplane but was looking forward to his flight. He said, "Nobody owes me anything, I owe them because I used the GI Bill to get my college degree. Just learn to be good at what you do."

As an Army artilleryman, Al Merkes served during the Korean War and beyond from February 1951 to January 1954. Merkes used a 155 howitzer and was assigned to patrol along the Russian border. He said, "Remember that the wall was still up." Merkes was joined by his wife, Bea, and daughters Michelle and Terri. He enjoyed his first open cockpit plane ride.

Homer Armagost of Waukesha, age 83, was another Korean War veteran. Armagost joined the California National Guard at age 16. He said, "Harry Truman thought I should see the Orient. I did for 19 months. It was so cold that fuel oil froze and all we had were summer uniforms. Our folks sent gloves and jackets from home. I got my first pair of winter shoes on the day I was coming home."

Trained as a map specialist, Armagost eventually hunted land mines by crawling along the roadway and probing the soil with his bayonet. "If I hit something hard," he said, "we used an explosive to blow it up later. Yes, we blew up some rocks. The Chinese mines held wooden boxes of picric acid. We had a tank flail apparatus for locating mines but since it was the only one in Korea, we used men to find the mines.

Men were expendable, that tank was not."

On to Northbrook, where Rockford's Aleck Johnson was the first dream flight recipient of the day. Johnson served with the Army Air Corps from 1943 to 1945 and was inducted on Pearl Harbor Day 1943 as an aviation cadet. Johnson said, "I was going to be a 90-day wonder but they didn't need me as a pilot."

Johnson did become a private pilot through the University of Illinois, flying his Cessna 172. He had never flown using a stick but talked with Darryl about flying the Stearman once they were in the air. Johnson declined to take control of the plane but did enjoy the flight. He said, "I can't believe how many trees there were, much like a forest. How can Darryl taxi without seeing where we are going?" Johnson's wife, Rosemary, attended the dream flight with him and recalled working on the atomic bomb.

As an ROTC graduate of the University of Illinois in 1954, Charles Sengstock served as a U.S. Army first lieutenant in Korea. He was the only one in his class of 150 who was sent directly to Korea. Sengstock said, "When they found out that I had radio broadcast experience, they had me run a gypsy (mobile) radio station. We flew a lot and in fact, I lived with a couple of pilots. Most of my flights were in spotter aircraft and Bell choppers. Once they asked me if I wanted to go into a spin on an L-19. I was young and single, so of course I did it." Discharged in 1956, Sengstock remained in the reserves for two more years.

Sengstock went to work for Chicago's WGN-TV in news and public relations. He met his wife, a film editor for WGN-TV, and they have now been married for 57 years. Sengstock had wanted to learn to fly but couldn't afford it. His wife, Norma, was on hand for the flight.

Following his dream flight, Sengstock said, "This was completely organized. All of your senses are alive. The noise, vibration, how the plane moves; it just makes you aware. It was everything I expected and more!"

Scott Lester from the control tower stopped by, himself a 20-year veteran of the Air Force. So did Krista Nordlund of Covenant Village, where most of the day's flyers lived. Darryl told them, "We want fingerprints on our planes. Most Stearman owners don't. And we are trained to work with the elderly, getting them in and out of the planes."

U.S. Marine Corps electronics technician Pete Anderson, 85, served from 1951 to 1953 during the Korean War but never was stationed overseas. Anderson was born in France, then lived in Iowa and New York state. He was excited about being in a small plane again with his last time being about 65 years ago. Anderson said, "The flight was as good as I thought it might be. I thought about all the guys in both wars who had to fly while trying to shoot someone down."

Anderson's wife, Rosemary, was the next to climb into the front seat of the plane. She was a nursing cadet during World War II, serving from 1942 to 1946. Rosemary met

Pete in Chicago when she went to a seminar on enjoying the single life. Rosemary said, "I am not really excited about flying." She changed her tune following the dream flight and asked her husband to buy one of these planes.

Another veteran with service in two wars was the next flyer. Tom Blim was a WWII veteran, serving from 1943 to 1947 as a Navy first lieutenant. He said, "I'm a Chicago boy. Most of our tour during the war was spent in the North Sea and the Red Sea. When called back for the Korean War, I was a deck officer and gunnery officer. Our purpose at the time was to show an American presence wherever we went."

Blim, 91, was joined by Joan, his wife of 63 years, and daughter Nancy Blim Young. He added, "I am not really that excited about flying and am glad that this plane is not going to have to land on a carrier with me in it, especially at night."

Retired Major General Cliff Clapp was on hand all day watching the proceedings and encouraging the veterans. He said, "I live at Covenant and I asked our nurse, Rita, if I should follow up the possibility of flying with Ageless Aviation Dreams Foundation. We agreed to call and see if they can come. That was four years ago. We do a lot with our veteran's group here, participating in the Memorial Day, Veteran's Day and Fourth of July events. I have been with the American Legion for 19 years."

General Clapp served in the U.S. Army from 1952 to 1955, then in the reserves from 1955 to 1962, then back to active duty in Vietnam before retiring in 1983. He was the first general to fly with AADF.

Drafted in 1971 near the end of the Vietnam War despite being in medical school, Jim Martins had already lost a good friend to the war in 1967. Martins served in the troop dispensary at Fort Ord, where hundreds came in sick each day. Trained in rapid response, Martins was one of 45 physicians assigned to the hospital emergency room. He volunteered to concentrate on general medicine, then began to specialize in cardiology. Martins said, "It was a great two years, I loved it and would do it again." He later served the veterans again at the VA Hospital in Iowa City, Iowa.

Martins, now 72, was accompanied by his wife, Sylvia. He had flown in helicopters with the doors removed so he had an unobstructed view of everything below. Following his flight, Martins said, "I enjoyed seeing the airport and Lake Michigan. It was wonderful being with Darryl, he certainly knows what he is doing."

Navy veteran Nick Kaup came with his wife, Mary, to experience his dream flight. Now 68, Kaup served in Naval Air Administration from 1966-1972, with highlights experienced both in Spain and at Guantanamo, Cuba. The Kaups continue to be active in American Legion and its auxiliary. Both are from Chicago. Following his flight, Mary Kaup said, "He's like a kid in a candy store." In fact, Nick Kaup knows a lot about the candy store. As sales manager for a national candy supplier, he later returned to the airport with a gift of candy samples for the AADF crew.

The last veteran flyer for the day was Craig Ardagh, age 58 from Chicago. Ardagh was a master sergeant in the Air Force, serving from 1976 to 2007. He specialized as a jet engine mechanic and in air transportation, performing weights and balances checks for cargo and personnel prior to their flights. Ardagh had flown in all the big cargo planes but never in a jet fighter. A highlight during his service was being aboard the plane that was refueling jets.

Ardagh asked Darryl if he could broadcast to the tower that the Stearman was ready for takeoff. "Sure, I believe we can make that happen," Darryl said. "I will coach you on what to say as we taxi out." Ardagh got his wish.

As a primary sponsor of the AADF, Signature Flight Support's Pam Kavanaugh said, "This is absolutely the best day of the year! Darryl says that he is lucky to work with us but the real truth is that we are even more lucky to be involved with honoring the selfless and sometimes forgotten heroes."

As often happens, Sport Clips had many volunteers on site. Nina Dietrich, Agnes Chavez, Krista Tianen, Melissa Bentley and Matt Camp helped the veterans enter and exit the plane. Dietrich said, "It is all about the people. It has been an emotional experience for all of us."

The plane and crew moved on to Steven's Point, Wisconsin, long hailed by Darryl and other AADF volunteers as one of the best tour stops each year. Plans had been underway for several years for Stevens Point to purchase its own Stearman plane and name it "The Spirit of Stevens Point." A pre-dream flight celebration was on tap complete with a ribbon cutting, an address by Wisconsin state Representative Katrina Shankland and various other civic and government officials, including Mayor Mike Wiza. Marcia McDonald led the event committee.

A huge crowd of flyers, family and well-wishers were on hand for the ceremony that honored the veterans along with Darryl and Bill's efforts to bring another AADF visit to Stevens Point. Refreshments and food were provided throughout the day.

First to fly was 92-year-old Eddie Lamken, who served in the Army Air Corps from 1943-45. Originally slated as an aviation cadet, Lamken's unit was moved to artillery and spent time in France and Germany. He said, "Nothing excites me anymore. But I got to kiss Marcia and that was nice. I did enjoy seeing lots of new things including the new expressway while we flew." Lamken's daughter Debbie and son David were on hand, along with Debbie's husband, Tom.

The next dream flight went to Jerry Bartosz, a nine-year Navy veteran. Much of his service was on aircraft carriers and shore patrol. Bartosz was accompanied by his wife, Kathleen, daughter Laura and son Tom. Bartosz said, "My overseas tour was the highlight of my service. I am very excited to fly because I have never been in an open cockpit plane." He also mentioned that Stevens Point was a diverse community with a rich history, settled predominantly by the Polish and filled now with wonderful people who keep the city clean.

After his flight, Bartosz said, "I saw my house twice. It was an incredible flight and more veterans need to do this."

Another veteran of carrier service was 83-year-old Tom Bredow. He served in the Mediterranean on the USS Midway and in the Caribbean on the USS Hornet. He was also on board the USS Bennington in 1954 when there was a big powder magazine explosion that resulted in 100 deaths and many more casualties. The ship limped back to Rhode Island and was eventually scrapped. With airplane maintenance responsibilities, Bredow worked primarily on the F9F Panthers and Cougars.

Bredow mentioned that while he was at home he heard the Stearman arriving because he was very familiar with the "snarl" of the engine. Bredow had some experience working on radial engines and loved the unique sound. He also said that many of the sailors on the carriers were divided into three categories, Airedales (flight crew), deck apes and snipes (those who worked below deck).

Yet another aircraft carrier veteran was George Nugent, having served in the Navy from 1941-43. Most of Nugent's service as a plane pusher was on the USS Midway, which had a crew of about 3,800 and was the first carrier of the historic Midway class. He also served on Lake Michigan.

The Navy took excursion boats and made them into small aircraft carriers. Nugent had a large family group on hand and with the help of Bredow, they learned much of Nugent's service history. They were so excited to hear these recollections that they videoed the talk, as they previously had heard little about Nugent's military experiences.

Another veteran with no open cockpit flight experience was 79-year-old Paul Horvath, a U.S. Marine from 1958-1963. He reached the rank of corporal while serving in Okinawa, Japan and Cuba. Horvath was especially proud that he had seen the famous Generals Chesty Puller and David Shoup.

Korean War Air Force veteran Richard Pike served from 1951-1955 as a dental assistant. Pike, age 83, had a deep interest in becoming a pilot but never got his wings. He saw a Wright Brothers plane replica fly and was especially proud of his hobby of building large model planes. Both of Pike's brothers served in the Army during WWII, one at Pearl Harbor and the other during the invasion of Okinawa. His only previous small plane ride was in a Piper Cub.

During his service in Army counterintelligence, Robert Knowlton had some unusual experiences. He worked in the Panama Canal Zone keeping track of the bad guys, the Soviets. Knowlton said, "We drove civilian cars and had to keep them spotless." Then Vice President Richard Nixon and his wife, Pat, visited Panama while Knowlton was on security detail. During his term of service from 1954-56, the president of Panama was assassinated.

Following his service, Knowlton used his GI Bill benefits to get his master's degree and doctorate and then taught 30 years at the University of Wisconsin at Stevens Point. Classes taught included US History, the French Revolution and Latin American History.

The fourth veteran of Naval carrier service was 91-year-old Terry Menzel. He served during WWII from 1943-46 as one of 5,000 sailors on the USS Franklin D. Roosevelt, part of a huge flotilla hunting German subs in the North Atlantic. The ship was not involved in any major battles during Menzel's service but was one of the first carriers to get jets.

Menzel said, "I have been so excited about flying today. It is something that I always wanted to do but I have never been in a plane. But the best part is that I don't have to be the pilot."

Army veteran William Olsen, age 81, served from 1954-58 and was the last dream flight recipient of the day. Two of his brothers served during WWII in the Navy. Olsen said, "I can't tell you what I did. I promised that years ago. But I have been a real fan of flying. This has been fascinating but I am not overwhelmed." Olsen was accompanied by his wife, Julie.

Following the dream flights at Stevens Point, some changes have been made as the city and county work to get their own Stearman biplane. Marcia McDonald reports that the committee is now headed by David Lamken, son of Eddie Lamken who took the first dream flight this year. David Lamken said, "My dad and I are both veterans but for some reason we had never been able to talk about his war experiences. Since his dream flight this year, dad had become a changed man. We now are able to talk openly about our service."

Lamken heads the newly named "Spirit of Wisconsin" committee which has set a goal of $125,000 to be raised during 2017 if possible. The name change provides outreach opportunities for increased funding. Mayor Wiza and Portage County employee leaders Patty Dreier and Stephanie Inman continue to support the effort. The plane will be based at Stevens Point but will tour as the other AADF planes do, enhancing the ability to get more veterans in the air throughout the Midwest.

Regular activities already scheduled include the annual Guns and Hoses softball game between the firemen and policemen and a fly-in to honor local veterans. A golf outing at the SentryWorld Golf Course and a kickoff dinner are both new for 2017.

CHAPTER 8

Batavia and Carol Stream, Illinois; back again and on to Decatur — September 6-8, October 13-14, 2016

I t was a bright and warm day on September 6 when the folks from Holmstead Assisted Living Center were scheduled to fly. Darryl was the pilot that day using the red and white 450 Stearman. The Dupage Airport facility near Batavia, Illinois, was first class with a huge tarmac and a fantastic main building.

Most of the flyers for that day arrived in the morning, planning to spend the day with AADF. The 2015 flight schedule for this group was rained out and the residents were glad to see good weather. Wes Ryd, an 86-year-old Air Force veteran, was a doctor at Fort Bragg and Pope Air Force base. Wes' wife, Lois, came along and was unaware that her husband was flying that day. They had been married 64 years and she said, "Oh, I am not surprised that he didn't tell me. That is just how he does things." To his credit, Wes wanted to make sure Lois came out to the plane to see him get in.

Before he went out to the tarmac, Ryd said that he had

not flown in anything like the Stearman and had only a few flights during his time in the Air Force. Wes remembered the case of a paratrooper who was snagged on the side of the plane by his harness. After several attempts to dislodge him that included a small plane flying underneath and trying to lift him up on the wing, the paratrooper was found dead when the transport plane returned to base.

Jim Crawford was an air traffic controller in the Air Force from 1951-53 and had six more years in the reserves. Jim, 84 years of age on his dream flight, was accepted into pilot training long enough to get one flight in a Stearman trainer. He said, "I washed out because my eyes were bad and it was the low point of my life. I became an air traffic controller because I couldn't see well enough but then told those who could see what to do."

Once when Jim was on leave, he asked if he could return to the base early. Jim was told that he didn't have to come back yet, but then replied, "Yes, I do. I am out of money."

A presentation of the colors was done just ahead of a short speech by State Representative Steven Andersson for the purpose of thanking all the veterans who were on hand. A luncheon followed for the veterans, their staff and any family members on hand.

Crawford waited to have lunch so that he could immediately get his dream flight underway and was returning when Darryl didn't see a small plane parked by itself as he taxied back to the exchange point. The Stearman propeller chewed up a small portion of the wing of the parked plane. The propeller was damaged along with part of the wing stabilizers. The airport fire truck came and offered support but there was little else for them to do.

After a short delay, the flyers for the rest of the day were told that there would be no more flights. Darryl quickly set about making the calls to AADF's insurance carrier, the FAA, a few experts concerning the Stearman and a couple of suppliers for parts. The disappointed flyers stopped by to ask a few questions and to offer their support to Darryl. The next two flyers in line had already been rained out the previous year and now would miss this day's flights. Both asked if it was possible to return this year or even early next year. Everyone concerned heard that it was just too early to tell at this point.

Eventually the damaged Cessna 206 plane was towed away, and the Stearman was taken to a hangar at the airport. Darryl had plans to get a repair expert in on the next day from the Stearman Fly-In at Galesburg, Illinois. He made arrangements to fly over from Galesburg on a friend's plane, define the needed repairs, and get them underway.

With the remaining schedule for the week disrupted, Darryl decided to drive to Galesburg. The ride from the Dupage airport took him through lots of older towns and rural areas on a scenic drive away from the crowded suburban areas.

The Stearman Fly-In took place for most of the week,

but Darryl only visited on September 7. First held in 1972, the fly-in once had as many as 141 planes in attendance. The 2016 version had about 50 planes on this day but more were expected by the weekend. Weather in other areas of the nation kept a few planes away. Still the numbers were respectable based on the fact that less than 1,000 planes remain from the 8,428 model Stearman 75s built as trainers for the U.S. Army and Navy. On a good year, the local economy receives a boost of about $500,000 from this event.

The purpose of Darryl's visit to the Stearman Fly-In was to offer an overview of AADF's mission and to generate interest in plane owners using their aircraft for veteran flights. In a scheduled presentation to the pilots, Darryl began with the latest AADF promotional video. In opening remarks, he talked about the veterans who board the AADF planes in their 80s and 90s, and get off with the smiles and quickened steps of someone at least 20 years younger.

Darryl continued with the statement, "My motivation is to get at least one of you to connect with your local veterans' organizations. We have an endorsement from the commander of the VFW and have a Joe Gibbs' fundraiser scheduled next week. I just want to do more! From a pilot's perspective, you've got to like people and embrace a sort of barnstorming." Darryl told them that the dream flight experience was a time to hear stories, listen to families, make hat presentations and get pictures afterwards.

Next up was a demonstration of how to load the veteran

into the plane, even those veterans with mobility issues. Darryl recounted some of the extreme loading successes from the past year but wanted the pilots to see how his process developed over the years. He said, "This is incredibly risky, but we are not going to let ethics interfere with our mission. We should not get sued for doing something good."

With that, Darryl completed the demonstration, and answered numerous questions about how anyone interested could take the next steps. Several pilots expressed interest and Darryl reminded them that the responsibility was theirs if they wanted to move forward.

Following some interesting conversations with other pilots and attendees at the fly-in, Darryl drove to Peoria for homeward bound flights while he continued to work on the possibility of repairs and whether a return to Dupage and the next scheduled flights in Decatur were possible.

Within a week, Darryl was able to arrange for the blue and yellow 1940 Stearman to be flown to Dupage with the flights scheduled for October 13 and 14. He made plans to return.

A few days later, Darryl found that he could not be there for the newly scheduled flights on Thursday, the 13th. He had a business meeting that couldn't be missed and those flights were to be picked up by Tim Newton, a newly certified Stearman pilot who would be heading the operation in Dupage this time around. Tim flies 777s for FedEx and was a fighter pilot in the Air Force.

Based on a chilly forecast, Tim expected that some of the flyers might not make it. This was Tim's first time leading the dream flights and he was ready to get it done. Tim left the hotel early and headed for Dupage to make the best of the day.

Five flyers from Holmstead were scheduled but only four of them arrived with the van. After a general introduction, 80-year-old Jim Perry was the first to head for the tarmac. He served in the Army from 1954 to 1956, of which about ten months were spent in school to learn Morse Code. Perry eventually became an instructor in Morse Code at Fort Sill. He said, "There were a few bad times, but I mostly enjoyed my time in service. I had a high draft number but volunteered ahead of that to get a better choice of service. This was just after Korea. Upon returning home, I went to school at the University of Illinois at Chicago's Navy Pier." Afterwards, Perry worked in research and was one of the flyers waiting to get airborne when the accident happened earlier.

Corporal Chuck Davis served in the Army at Fort Belvoir, Virginia as a company clerk. Davis, 87, did reports for MPs because he had a college degree and could type. With his service during 1951-1953, Davis spent lots of time listening to Chosen Reservoir vets coming home from Korea. His dad fought in WWI and worked for the FBI and his brother was a Navy photographer on the USS Saratoga during WWII.

Davis had possibly the quote of the day when he landed safely after his dream flight and said, "Back on the ground, no inheritance!"

Corporal Wayne Glassman joined Perry as return flyers from the last two aborted AADF trips. Glassman, 87, was responsible for various training, plus a drill team and softball and football teams while his real work came from providing maintenance on a fleet of "mothball ships." All of this happened in Stockton, California while Glassman served from 1956-58.

Former Army corporal Karl Pierson, 87, worked during the Korean Conflict as an instructor at the U.S. Armed Forces Institute where he taught those who needed GEDs. He said, "I was just in the right place at the right time and served stateside even though I had no experience as a teacher." Pierson did not arrive with the other veterans earlier in the morning because his nurse said that he couldn't go fly. After a conversation with at least one Holmstead administrator, the nurse reversed her stance and allowed Pierson to attend.

A former plane owner, Pierson is now confined to a wheelchair but added, "I just wanted to fly one more time. I love flying!" With help from the firefighters on hand, Pierson was able to get in the plane and achieve that dream.

Lowell Nordling, then 85, also served in the Army during the Korean Conflict as an armored infantry instructor.

He said, "I worked with the National Guard and regular recruits on infantry problems. Working with the recruits was much better because the National Guard guys were only with us for a week and then were gone." Nordling never went overseas, although he was on a plane about to leave for a foreign theatre when the flight was canceled.

Later, Nordling worked with the chaplain's office and helped with supplies. Originally from Minnesota, his family convinced him to move to Illinois for his retirement. Although Nordling had never flown in a Stearman, he remembers as a youngster seeing them used as crop dusters and the excitement of a plane landing in nearby hayfields.

Nordling was the last Holmstead flyer. Firemen Tom Cote and Jeff Gove assisted with loading veterans with mobility issues and Sport Clips employees on hand were Mercedes Clarke, Kristy Kanwischer and Natalie Isakson. Becky and Ellyn were on hand from the Holmstead staff, with Becky attending on her day off. She said, "I just had to come see it all."

The afternoon group of veterans came from Windsor Park. They arrived at about noon and Tim kept flying with only brief bathroom breaks because he had been notified to return to work after the day's dream flights were completed. Tim would leave and Darryl would arrive overnight, leaving Darryl as the pilot in charge for the next day.

Back to the afternoon flights. First flyer for the group was Al Bossert who served in the Army between Korea and

Vietnam, from 1956 to 1958. He was an instructor in radar fundamentals and mortar trajectory. An interesting sideline was Bossert's responsibility for taking care of carrier pigeons. He said, "Yes, we still used them and we had parades when one would die." Born and raised in the Chicago area, Bossert once took apart a radial engine similar to the one that powered the Stearman.

Another Army veteran was Ray Smith. Drafted after the Korean War, he served from 1956-58 and then had four years in the reserves. Smith worked in the Pentagon for nine months processing the paperwork for generals who were retiring. He said, "I was a professional journalist who became the editor of the post newsletter at Fort McNair, home of the National War College. It was voted the best newsletter in our district." Smith recalled that Fort McNair was the site of the hanging of the conspirators from Abraham Lincoln's assassination.

Discharged in 1962 with the rank of SP-5, the equivalent of sergeant, Smith recounted his memories of growing up on Pearl Harbor. He did not see the aerial bombardment of December 7 but described the aftermath of a Jap Zero running out of fuel. The pilot shot one of the Hawaiians, then was beaten to death in return. Up to 10,000 American troops were eventually stationed near Smith's boyhood home.

Navy veteran Ed Dasbach served on a destroyer as a machinist mate for most of 1953 to 1957. The destroyer Tingey was part of a fleet of ships that went to Thailand and once had a standoff with a Chinese submarine. Dasbach became a pilot after his service and owned a Piper Cherokee. Dasbach said, "I loved flying, especially takeoffs and landings. I really enjoyed my military service and should have stayed in." Born and raised in Chicago, he has lived the last 47 years in Bloomingdale and Carolstream, Illinois.

While most of the day's veterans had seen little or no overseas action, Dom Errichiello had been right in the middle of the fighting from Normandy on to Germany during WWII. An Army veteran, Errichiello went ashore on the third wave of the D-Day invasion of Omaha Beach. He said, "The first two waves were almost complete suicide. We had no choice but to step over dead bodies. I actually hid behind them for a short while. Our group had to climb the cliffs by grabbing tree roots to take out the pillboxes."

Errichiello was captured along with eight other American soldiers by seven Germans at the Battle of the Bulge. One of the men understood enough German to know that they would soon be shot. All nine ran in different directions and only two survived, Errichiello and his lieutenant. He added, "I went from one battle to another, went to Berlin and saw the holocaust. I will never forget those things." Medals awarded included the Silver Star, the Bronze Star and the Purple Heart.

Following the dream flight, Errichiello was even more outspoken. He enjoyed bantering with Tim and visiting with the Sport Clips girls and local media.

The final flyer for the day was Lee Heft, an Army 11th Airborne veteran who served in the Japan occupation army from 1946-1947. He said, "There were many scars and signs of the war. Our basic job was cleaning up bombed out factories. The culture was very different over there." Heft learned to parachute in Japan and had to make a jump every three months to stay certified. Originally from Chicago, Heft and his wife Nancy have been married 63 years.

Windsor Park Life Enrichment Coordinator Adrian Ursache closed out the day by saying, "What a blessing is this once in a lifetime opportunity! The joy and satisfaction is so apparent after they land, you can tell that they love it."

Tim and Darryl did swap out overnight, leaving Darryl to fly the plane to Decatur early on the next morning. A light frost covered the area and no one relished the thoughts of cold weather open cockpit flying. A chilly flight of nearly two hours over beautiful farmland ended with the arrival at Decatur to a standing ovation from soon-to-be flyers and plenty of spectators.

The first flyer on October 14 was 92-year-old Army Sergeant Emmitt Gaffron who served from 1943 to 1946. His principal duty was as fire chief guarding a refinery on Curacao.

Next up was Jim Hurd, an Army Korean War veteran who served in an artillery observation battalion. He said, "The first bunch of guys had it rough over there. The winter was brutal and over 8,000 men are still unaccounted for. There was a lot of bunker and trench warfare. And our equipment was mostly World War II stuff."

Hurd's wife Alicia, son James, daughter Judy and her husband, Mark all attended. Hurd said after the flight, "I see why people take up flying!"

Radio and electronics Air Force veteran John Blair, then 83, was a staff sergeant and part of the Strategic Air Command. Blair instructed pilots in the use of auto-pilot and flew on planes such as the B-24, B-25 and B-56. The B-56 had ten engines, 6 props and 4 jets.

Blair was accompanied by his daughter, Judy Blair-Myers. Blair said, "I keep looking straight at Darryl and all I see is his chest." When asked if he was ready to fly, Blair replied, "Crank 'em up!"

Merchant Marines veteran Ivan Wiley at 90-years-old had served by maintaining 20mm anti-aircraft guns while his ship went to Europe, Russia and Belgium. Wiley was also responsible for radar, lookouts and gun control. He said, "We had to be alert at all times. We saw buzz bombs and were told not to shoot at them. We wanted them to keep flying out of the area. While the Germans held out in Belgium, we saw the British Stearman planes looking for mines and subs."

Always a resident of Decatur, Wiley lost a son, Richard Dennis Wiley in Vietnam. Richard Wiley was a gunner in a helicopter. Ivan Wiley remembered, "The last time I saw him was at this airport. His service was more honorable than mine."

Steve Nichols, the cameraman for WAND, NBC 17 on hand to cover the event, was also an Air Force veteran in Para rescue. He took shrapnel in his back, landed on a rock and his back was broken after being shot on the way down. Nichols served from 1987-94 and has since recovered from his injuries.

Perhaps one of the most memorable veterans of the day was Jack Sutherland, Jr. Sutherland fought in the Air Force from 1964-65 and was stationed at the Tan Son Nhut Air Base in Saigon. He said, "I feel bad about all the guys who were killed and have trouble shaking the sadness. There were just a lot of sad memories. I remember going to Saigon one night and the next night the particular area was bombed."

Sutherland was joined by his wife Doris as he waited for his flight. He added, "I was hoping I could do this. It is my only chance to fly and it means a lot." Sutherland, a lifelong Decatur resident, was confined to a wheelchair but able to get into the plane with only minor difficulty.

Upon his return, Sutherland said, "I enjoyed my time in the service but this flight was one of the greatest experiences of my life. How wonderful!"

Tyfanni Allen was the Sport Clips representative on hand and took special pride in the day's experience. Very pregnant, Tyfanni had no trouble climbing the wing to strap in the veterans and took many pictures of her own.

Another Army veteran, Lloyd Aukamp, served in Germany in the motor pool parts room from 1953-55. He said, "I went to Paris and saw the beautiful city. I enjoyed watching the girls. Pretty city, but they didn't like us much." On the way home, Aukamp remembers that one of the engines quit but his flight arrived safely.

Mary Leming was the next to fly. Leming, 79, had lived in Decatur her entire life. She brought her daughter Carla, son Carl and son-in-law Steve to see her fly. A past world traveler, Leming listed Greece as her favorite destination country. Leming also said, "I have another daughter, Darla, and if Carl had been a girl, he was going to be Marla."

With the quote of the day, Leming was about to get in the plane when a wind gust nearly blew Darryl's hat off. When his hands left Leming, she said, "Don't drop my ass to save your hat!"

Though no relation to Darryl, Brunhilde Fischer was the next flyer. Then 92½ years of age, Brunhilde grew up in Germany during WWII and lived near Stuttgart. She said, "I bet someone in Darryl's family changed his name years ago, otherwise he would still spell it like mine. I had five brothers who served in the German army. A sixth was about to go and the mayor got him a deferment. I didn't have to go either because I had cows and parents at home to take care of. I was one of 14 brothers and sisters and am the only one left."

"I have been waiting three years to do this. I flew in Germany but this is my first time flying since 1962. I last visited Germany then and had a sister who I never met until I moved to America. That was in March, 1957."

Fischer remembered the almost never-ending air raids of Allied planes during WWII, sometimes as many as 500 at a time overhead. Once, she saw the bombs falling. Fischer said, "I could always tell if they had dropped their bombs or not, because the planes would just be lumbering along when the bombs were still on board and much faster afterwards."

Resident Melvin Clary was especially thankful for his chance to fly. His mother was a WWII WAC (Women's Army Corp) and his dad served in the Army artillery. Clary said, "I like to go on trips, and my favorite is going to Hooters!" Known for being helpful to other residents, Clary added, "I love to fly but this is my first time in a small plane."

Flora May Andes was the last flyer of the day. She had three sons, one Army and two Marines, who joined her WWII Army husband in a military family. Born and raised in Decatur, she said, "My second time flying is today. I am going to bring up the rear end today!" Andes was known as an avid church worker and a great cook.

With that, the flights concluded for this odyssey that covered about three weeks. Lori Terrell, life enrichment coordinator, said, "For these veterans, this is a step back in time for them and they certainly deserve the recognition. They made and are still making such a significant contribution to the world that we live in today."

The plane was ferried back to Atlanta over the next two days to continue its own dream flight schedule.

CHAPTER 9

Oxford, Mississippi;
The 2,000th flight — October 27, 2016

eturning to the site of the first flight for a soon-to-be-developed Ageless Aviation Dreams had been in the planning stages since 2015. That first flight came about because of a long list of unique opportunities, not so much a series of coincidences but something that was just "meant to be."

Bill Fisher had restored a Stearman plane in Cleveland, Mississippi, and needed to ferry it home. Because of Darryl's work issues at the time, he was available to help fly it but had little money. Darryl told his father, "I would love to go with you, but you will have to pay the bills!" A fuel stop in Oxford, Mississippi, provided the opportunity to take a veteran for a flight, the first.

The Brookdale Assisted Living facility in Oxford had once been part of Darryl's nursing home holdings. But that was no longer the case. Knowing that the airport there would be the first fuel stop, he called Director Sandra Enfinger and asked her to set up that first flight with a veteran. Enfinger chose Mr. Newton and said, "He was a jolly fellow, but he had dementia. His wife traveled by wheelchair and fussed at him constantly in a very cute way. Every time I saw them, I would ask how was the happy couple. They would both chuckle. That is what Mr. Newton did all the time."

Mr. Newton was so excited, just as the other veterans are when they get the chance to fly. He did have a lot of questions and then he wanted to talk about his work taking care of a runway during the WWII. Mr. Newton's job was to light up the runway when he heard the planes coming. One night, he heard planes coming and it was the enemy, so he quickly turned the lights off.

Enfinger was not sure as to what exactly would happen at the airport. She just knew that Darryl and his father were flying to Oxford in an open cockpit plane. Enfinger added, "I am sure that it was comical how I described the adventure to Mr. and Mrs. Newton and their son. I told them that my friends were coming and they wanted to take a veteran for a ride."

While the Brookdale residents waited on the bus, they said things like, "Where are they? Are you sure they are still coming?" Mr. Newton was excited and giddy, with Mrs. Newton fussing and laughing at the same time.

Suddenly, Enfinger heard Darryl's voice on the airport radio. She said, "It was absolutely wonderful to hear his voice. Darryl was Darryl, very genuine. He put Mr. Newton in the plane and off they went for the flight. When they returned, Mr. Newton was so excited and hugged me, then gave me a kiss on the cheek. I told him that he had better go give his sweet wife a kiss. I always remember this day with a smile on my face. It was a fantastic day and I'm so grateful that we were Darryl's first flight!"

Steve Toma was Brookdale's second flight. "He was a tall, slim man and a big talker," Enfinger said. "He gladly told his story and he told it a lot. My favorite memory of the flight is when Mr. Toma and Darryl made their Roseburg, Oregon, connection. I also remember waiting for the landing and to see his reaction. It was kind of like a wedding … looking to see the groom's reaction when he sees the bride walking down the aisle. When he got off the plane, Mr. Toma had tears in his eyes as he was so overwhelmed by the excitement and very thankful to Darryl."

After the flight, Toma announced that he and Darryl were previously neighbors back in Washington State. Mr. Toma knew Darryl's father. Enfinger said, "Mr. Toma and Darryl were laughing and talking about Roseburg, at least Mr. Toma was talking. Darryl told Mr. Toma that he would come back and give another flight on his 100th birthday."

Brookdale Sales Manager Lori Hannah added, "The flight was all Mr. Toma could talk about for days. I helped him type up his story and I bet I wrote three or four drafts until it was perfect. Mr. Toma wore his hat that Darryl had given him almost every day. He was so proud that he had been chosen to be a part of the dream flights."

The 2016 visit from AADF involved Darryl and Bill again. But the celebration was much bigger this time, complete with a formal ceremony. As part of the program, Darryl recounted the original visit and how it came about. He said, "Dad was here, paying the bills. Without him, none of this would have happened. From this little seed planted, we are giving our 2,000th flight today. These flights are so pure, a huge treat to the veterans and our volunteers. Every day that we fly these veterans, I tear up at something."

"On the way back home during that first trip, we gave 25 more free flights. Now as we are about to do the 2,000th flight, we operate because of generous donations and support. Thanks to Sport Clips, our other sponsors and multiple veterans' organizations and today the fire department and police department."

Enfinger introduced the veterans who were being honored on this special day. She remembered, "Mr. Newton was so tickled to be the first flyer and then Darryl came back and took up Mr. Toma. Darryl and Mr. Toma realized that they were neighbors at one time in Roseburg. I know that all of our veterans today will have special memories from their own flight."

Local pastor Fish Robinson offered the prayer, but an unusual one because he asked everyone to pray with their eyes open. He said, "When I think of this generation of men and women, I think of one word. Sacrifice! God broke the mold with them. We have not forgotten them and offer our gratitude. God is not through with these men yet and I ask your blessing for them as well as the pilots and rest of the AADF volunteers, along with those at Brookdale. God, please help us understand their sacrifice as they leave their legacy. God, please show up and show out!"

With that, the flights began. Angus Emerson was the first flyer. Emerson was a first lieutenant in the Army who served at Homewood, Illinois. His unit was responsible for guarding Chicago with surface-to-air missiles known as the Nike Hercules. The medium and high altitude long-range missiles stood ready to be used at any time. These missiles were never fired but Emerson did get to fire two missiles while training at White Sands, New Mexico. As executive officer, Emerson's duties included security, safety, pay, supply and R&R. Emerson said, "I had about ten titles, but one of the main things was I got a check each payday that had to be divided out to all the men. I carried a 45 pistol but had never been trained to use it. They had me burn secret and confidential papers in a drum on occasion."

AADF volunteer and pilot Tim Newton was the ground crew for this day so he got to position Emerson in the plane. Newton said, "Mr. Emerson, would you like us to strap you in or not? We don't want any unplanned departures." Emerson, who was quite talkative, said, "I never got a whipping in school for cheating but I got it for talking. You really got to know what you are doing to strap us in, don't you?"

After the 20-minute flight with Darryl at the controls,

Emerson had more to say. "If you tried to jump out, you couldn't even if you wanted to. Do I get to go up and walk on the wings now? It was a lot better than I expected." Emerson, 79 years of age, was accompanied to the airport by his sister, Betty.

The next flyer, 93-year-old Lloyd Smith, was an Army Air Corps staff sergeant during World War II. Smith was serving as a ball turret gunner on a B-17 when the plane was shot up during an air raid over Brunswick, Germany. They crashed into the ocean 23 miles from Belgium. Smith said, "We saw a plane coming over and starting flashing our lights toward it. Turned out it was a German plane and pretty soon a German boat came and picked us up."

The Germans took the crew to a Dutch town and put them into a dungeon where they spent three or four nights. Then they were loaded into a small boxcar and taken with others by train very slowly across Belgium to Austria. Smith's group arrived in Krems, Austria, and was taken to Stalag 17B Prison Camp where they spent the next 12½ months of their lives.

Eventually, with the war coming to an end, the Austrian and German guards took the 2,200 men out of the camp and walked them across Germany for 3½ weeks. Smith said, "We were in a big hurry because the guards knew that the Russians were coming. Those guards treated us well but one of the guards kicked me and it took out three people. I was so cold. My nerves were shot by the time we left the

POW camp."

At Brenau Woods near Hitler's birthplace, the column stopped to camp for three to four days before Patton's Third Army liberated them. The POWs were taken to Camp Lucky Strike in an effort to put some weight on them before being sent home.

Smith's flight was similar to the others that day. They flew over Oxford and the nearby University of Mississippi football stadium. Upon his return, Smith said, "The landing was real smooth. It was the first time I had seen Oxford from the air and was surprised at how many trees we have. I know this type of plane was a favorite of crop dusters. We had lots of cotton and beans in the Delta."

Smith's wife of 62 years, Martha, his daughter Marissa and niece McKenzie were all on hand for the flight. Martha said, "I know he is happy!" Marissa added, "He looked cool as a cucumber. You got him back down. It's over now, we can breathe."

During the hat ceremony, Darryl asked Smith to reverse the usual roles and sign his hat. Darryl said, "You are my hero and I'd like you to sign my hat." Smith had just received AADF's 2,000th flight.

With the next flyer aboard and in the sky, Smith added a few more thoughts as he sat back and thought over the experience. "I was a little apprehensive about today," he said. "It's a big day and I appreciate the honor of letting me be the 2,000th flyer. It wasn't a surprise because Lori told me.

We have such a capable staff at Brookdale."

As almost an afterthought, Smith said, "I want to thank the Red Cross for what they did for us during World War II. We were extremely fortunate to have the eight-pound parcel of food each week. The Germans only fed us a weak soup once a day. The package included powdered milk chocolate, concentrated lemons and coffee. By the end of our time in the camp, we only had one package for eight men."

Earnest "Ernie" Aune, 88, was an Air Force sergeant from 1951-1954. Aune was an air traffic controller and also did radar ground control when he served in Anchorage, Alaska. The primary planes that he was responsible for were F-89s. Aune flew with an uncle in a Piper Cub and once flew in a B-29 when going from one base to another, but had never flown in an open cockpit plane.

Aune said, "I really enjoyed my time in the Air Force and should have continued in air traffic control as a civilian. I never had an accident." Aune was joined by his two sons, Eddie and David, both born in Anchorage.

After his flight, Darryl told Aune that he had two handsome sons, to which Aune replied, "Yes, they are but the main subject might not be." When Darryl gave Aune his hat, Aune asked, "Does this get me another ride next year?"

With all the flights complete for the day and the residents on the way back to Brookdale Oxford, Enfinger said, "I will never forget the day when Darryl called and wanted to start this adventure. I am so thankful to him for letting us be the first and 2,000th flight. When I worked for Darryl, it was always about the senior adults. He encouraged us then to make dreams come true for them, small and large. Now Ageless Aviation is making dreams come true for our veterans."

After the completion of the flights in Oxford, Darryl and his dad headed by car to the Columbus Air Force Base in Columbus, Mississippi. Tim followed in the Stearman after completing some paperwork and fueling. With Tim's help, Darryl had a great chance of getting a flight in a training jet but the deal was not yet done. He needed to be at the base by 3 p.m. and complete some more of the pre-flight requirements.

Tim had submitted the request for flights for himself and Darryl in the spring of 2016. The AFB had a change of command requiring resubmission of the requests. Darryl said, "I had received a call from Captain David Hoffman who informed me that I had been pre-approved for the incentive flight but that he needed more information. After a number of questions and some additional paperwork, Captain Hoffman asked me whether I was a dignitary, elected official or former military. When I had to answer no to all of them, he told me that it would be tough to get further approval."

This conversation happened about two weeks prior to the possible date for the flight, prompting Darryl to dismiss the idea. However, nine days prior to the flight, Captain Hoffman called back, saying, "You have been approved through this section but more information was still needed and that it would be obtained upon your arrival. It is still not a done deal." Another call, just two days prior to the event, asked for Darryl's estimated time of arrival.

"When we got to the AFB on Thursday, October 27, about 3 p.m., we realized that they really rolled out the red carpet for us. Tim and Dad got to come with me to see and experience the event which made this extra special to me. They had passes ready and were set to show us around," said Darryl. After an extensive session of orientation and ground training which had included getting Darryl's equipment ready, the initial session was completed about 6 p.m. Darryl was fitted with a flight suit, boots, G-suit, helmet and gloves. The G-suit took about 20 minutes because it had multiple adjustments, including the oxygen valves. Total time for the equipment preparation was about one hour.

Before Darryl could fly, he needed approval by a flight surgeon after a full medical evaluation. "I was concerned about that because my size or height/weight ratio that included 240 pounds of body weight was over the limitation to fly in the back seat," Darryl said. "I needed to be in the back seat and a commander's signature was required to waive it to get final approval. They found the base commander, got his signature and we were set to fly."

With the flight scheduled for 12:30 p.m. the next day,

Darryl was instructed to arrive by 7:15 a.m. The time in between was used for additional training, including G-forces, hydrology, proper breathing, how to help blood flow during G-force flying and use of the ejection seat. Darryl added, "I had to get in the ejection seat in the classroom to learn the nine points where I would connect once inside the jet. We learned the emergency procedures in case we needed to eject and the seat or canopy doesn't open correctly or if something got twisted. We talked about different scenarios and what to do in each. I actually got in the harness and learned how to land should I need to eject. Points covered included how to position my feet and how to collapse my body, among other things. I never imagined that the pre-flight training would be so detailed."

The ejection seat has two pins that must be pulled as the jet taxied out. The pilot instructor decided when to remove them. The ejection seat is a safety measure both for when in the air but also while on the ground with no altitude or air speed. The first pin, red in color, is located between your legs. The other is attached to a lever to the left of seat that actually arms the ejection mechanism.

After training, Darryl was instructed to change into his flight suit and helmet. He said, "We had laid all of this out last night. They let Tim come out on the flight line to talk to me and help with the suit. I learned that the flight would be an actual training flight. There would be two planes, one with me and my instructor and another used for instructor training." The "student" pilot in the other plane would actually sit in the back seat and watch what the instructor did in the front seat. The "student" was required to catch his mistakes.

During the pre-flight briefing, lasting about 45 minutes, different aspects of the mission were discussed. The mission would include nine bombing runs of different varieties and three strafing runs. The "student" led the briefing while the instructor questioned him and often would say incorrect things to see if the "student" caught and corrected the mistakes. Darryl said, "It was helpful to watch this but I think I only understood about 30 percent because there was a lot of military language and situations. It was all very different than flying civilian but I did understand the mission and most of what to expect."

With the flight about to take place, Darryl was apprehensive. He said, "I was nervous about my height/weight ratio being approved. I also knew that the G-forces would be pretty intense and was worried about getting sick. There was nothing that I could do except practice my breathing as they had taught me the day before. I also knew from instructions that I could use the switch to breathe pure oxygen which helps with air sickness if I ever did get to feeling bad. Tim had prepped me ahead of time to help me calm down."

An extensive procedure was required to prepare to taxi. Darryl recounted, "There was a crew chief and a lot of preparation, and the difference between military and civilian was dramatic. I had nine different things to hook my G-suit into and more for communications. It took us about 20 minutes to get ready to taxi. I was worried that I wouldn't fit into the cockpit because I sit really high. My goal was to be able to fit my hand between my helmet and the canopy. By lowering the seat as far as it would go, my spacing was perfect."

The instructor pilot fired up the jet and taxied out to do a formation take off. He showed Darryl how to taxi and was instructed to pull the button on the stick to activate the rudders in order to taxi. Darryl said, "Then you let the button go for the jet to go straight. It was very sensitive and I never got the hang of it. My instructor took over. Then the runways were very busy and we had to taxi across one to get to ours for take-off. We were lead jet on the take-off and we used the after-burners which really sets you back in the seat."

Once off the ground and with the after-burners turned off, the ride was quiet and smooth as the jet traveled at 350 knots. The bombing range was 70 miles away. Darryl flew the jet while in formation, about three to four jet widths off the right wing of the other jet. Very quickly, the two jets reached the bombing range. The instructor flew the first bombing run and then asked Darryl if he wanted to fly the second. Darryl was hesitant but agreed and reached 420 knots before rolling out onto the target at 1,000 feet above the ground. Darryl said, "The instructor kept telling me to 'pull' because at that speed you have to turn tight and bank it at 90 degrees, otherwise the jet will quickly drift way off the course. He would tell me that the airplane was mine and would correct our position. I also had a hard time figuring where to roll out because I couldn't see the other jet very well. Every turn would be pulling about five Gs and the jet was shaking because it was at the edge of a stall. We were maxing the jet, just exactly what needed to happen. The first turn I flew was horrible but I got better. I had a hard time figuring my points of reference and the instruments for air speed and other readings I needed were in different locations."

The instructor always dropped the "bombs," which were actually all electronic-simulated with lasers. His results came up on the instrument display to show how close he was to the target. After strafing, the jet flew at a 30-degree angle turn while our air speed was 420 knots. "It's mind boggling since everything you are doing requires working very hard. Keeping track of the other jet, looking for your target and watching the instruments all required your full attention. We hardly ever flew straight because we were always turning," added Darryl.

Standard routine requires a damage assessment. Darryl's jet pulled up on the left side of the other jet to inspect it and then continued underneath and finally to its right side to continue the assessment. Then the roles reversed as the other jet returned the favor.

On the way back to the base, the instructor pilot gave Darryl control once again but had to take it back when they lost sight of the other jet. Colonel Drown told Darryl that he was too high and too far forward and quickly pulled hard on the stick, which slowed the aircraft down and turned it upside down. Darryl said, "I asked him why he did that. I was told that by slowing the jet down and going inverted, we could get him back in sight. We got into tight formation on the way back. The other jet was so close, I felt like I could reach out and touch it. The details on the screw heads were easily seen, which made me very uncomfortable."

Darryl continued, "Colonel Drown was very complimentary of my flying, but I don't know if he was just being nice. I had no idea how I did but I flew about half the mission, just under an hour. Once we landed, I had lots of feelings. I was bummed that Tim didn't get to fly but it was wonderful having Tim and Dad there as support and to share the moment. I was excited because this was an amazing experience, a chance of a lifetime! After the flight, I didn't feel good. I was exhausted because it was a very intense one hour. I don't think it was the G-forces but rather simply the release of anticipation and intensity of the experience. It was fascinating to see what military pilots really do to train and gave me a glimpse into a completely new world."

Just a few words from Tim put Darryl's flight in perspective. Tim spent 18 years at Columbus as an instructor pilot, eight of those years in a T-37 and ten in a T-38. The rest of his 26 years in the Air Force were spent as a combat pilot and as an instructor in the F-16. Colonel Drown was the commander of the 43rd Reserve Squadron at Columbus AFB.

"Darryl's approval to fly had to come from the Chief of Staff of the Air Force, General David Goldfein, the guy in charge of the whole Air Force! Our ace in the hole was that we had given his dad, Colonel Goldie Goldfein, a dream flight in San Antonio on Veteran's Day 2015. So, I think General Goldfein knew who we were. From all reports, Darryl did a fantastic job in the jet," said Tim.

Tim concluded with comments often said by those individuals who are fortunate to get the incentive flights: "I didn't realize how much preparation was required, I didn't realize how much you have to know and I didn't realize how physical it is to fly these jets. And finally, I'm tired and I want to go take a nap!" Those words were very similar to what Darryl had just said after his feet were back on the ground.

CHAPTER 10

Jacksonville, Fort Myers and Kissimmee, Florida,
with Mike and Diane — November 8-11, 2016

C haplain and Captain Patrick J. McCormack was the opening speaker for a rowdy celebration prior to the dream flights on November 8, 2016, in Jacksonville, Florida. He said, "My first flight ever was in a Stearman, but the straps were so loose that they wouldn't have held me in."

Attired in his dress uniform, Captain McCormack said, "You folks will be kings and queens for a day. Wilbur Wright once said that flying is a perfect peace mixed with nerve straining excitement. Our veterans have served a cause larger than oneself, and 2.2 million of you have served in our armed forces. We must defend our freedom; if left undefended, it can easily be taken away."

The celebration concluded with lunch, just in time for pilot Mike Winterboer to taxi the blue and yellow Stearman in place for loading the first flyer of the day. The flyers were residents of Arbor Terrace. The morning had been filled with hustle and intrigue as Winterboer and mechanic

Karl Gratiex picked up a replacement propeller at FedEx in hopes of mounting it on the plane in time to start the afternoon's flights. The group had a van to transport the propeller and had to do a little remodeling of the console area to make it fit. Karl seemed equally adept at reworking the van as he was with working on planes. When it looked like the long wooden box might not fit, a final shove allowed the rear door to snugly close. The FedEx supervisor watched with a smile and said, "Oh, well, it is just a rental!"

After hustling back to the airport, the men found themselves short of tools and had to make a quick run to Sears. With just minutes to spare, the propeller was properly mounted and all was well. Sport Clips had a crew on hand that included Cristin Kelley, Carissa Romero, LaTeeka Bowens, Samantha Graham, Morgan Malloy and Argentina Trevino. This group had volunteered from the six stores in Jacksonville and were just closing out their own "Help a Hero" program.

Gratiex had been working with AADF almost since the foundation's beginning. He said, "I had always enjoyed aviation and built my own helicopter. If Darryl wanted something, I would do my best to get it done. I would like to develop a maintenance program now that the organization has grown so much in hopes of streamlining and planning services ahead of time."

Veterans were ready to fly and quickly Mike and Diane got the show on the road. First to take to the air was

90-year-old Ben Allen, former chief petty officer and Navy gunner. Ben didn't talk much, but did say, "I am not old. I will drag myself into that plane if I have to!" Allen served in the Navy from 1943 to 1964.

Jerome "Jerry" Orr was a 79-year-old Navy veteran from 1959-1966. He said, "I flew planes and helicopters but it is easier to fly a plane than a helicopter. The larger the helicopter, the harder it is to fly." President Nixon once needed a helicopter and Jerry was available, but the staff would not allow Nixon to board, saying, "No President is ever going to fly on that!"

Orr worked in finance post-service, including some time on Wall Street in New York City. His post-military work took him from California to New York and then to Florida. When Orr was about to take off, the crowd cheered and chanted, "Good luck to Jerry! Go Jerry!"

Future AADF pilot Bob Brodie joined the ground crew for the rest of the afternoon flyers. Brodie currently was on active duty in the Marines as a fighter pilot and would become part of the pilot rotation in 2017.

The next flyer was a veteran of both the Marine Corps and the Merchant Marines. Edward "Poppi" Kissam was joined on this day by his significant other, BJ. Kissam told Brodie, "Once a Marine, always a Marine!" Kissam, who was 91, remembered a day as a Merchant Marine when his ship was in port but was told to move to another berth. When another ship moored into Kissam's previous birth, it was bombed. He was assigned to a 100mm gun on the ship but never fired it. Later, he became a navigator on a bomber.

After his service, Kissam became the first orthopedic surgeon in Gainesville, Florida, and was the team doctor for the Florida Gators. Before his service, Kissam had been offered a full scholarship to play football for Clemson University but declined the offer.

Arbor Terrace Engagement Director Mike Kaminski said, "We hope to get more flights in the spring. Just giving these residents the chance for spontaneous living, complete with the sights and sounds of an airfield, is a huge victory for them. Often their life is full of anxiety and fear but they are still proud and distinguished. They will be sharing this experience for quite a while, an experience that not many get."

A non-veteran flyer took to the air next. Mada Allen was the first saleswoman for Florida Power and Light and once ran a plow company. She said, "I was also a schoolteacher for 15 years and one of my students was football great Pat Summerall."

Another Arbor Terrace staff member said she spent plenty of time in airplanes as a flight attendant for 20 years. Tracy Bass also said her son would leave for the Army on January 6, 2017. "I love spending time with the veterans," she added. "They have so many stories and they nearly always come back to their times in service. Any time that we can give them a moment to reminisce is well spent."

Mallorie Collyer, in charge of the event for Arbor Terrace, said, "This day has been absolutely amazing! The residents forgot that they are old. For one day, they were young again."

The flight crew moved on the next day to Ft. Myers where Ernie Sweeney was the first flyer. He was born in Piedmont, Missouri, and brought his daughters, Diane and Tricia. They had arranged for a surprise flight with AADF after their dad saw some old planes at the same airport recently.

The 80-year-old Sweeney remembered that he grew up flying "pretty much what they gave me." He said, "Once I looked back at dad in the back seat of the airplane and said, 'hey, look at this.' Then I threw the stick out. Of course it was a fake stick!"

Serving as a pilot from 1954 to 1974, Sweeney flew in Korea and Vietnam and during five wars with Israel. Once, when flying a twin-engine Grumman, he had to eject through the skin of the plane before being picked up by a Jolly Green Giant, the 834 helicopter. Another crewman was rescued out of a tree.

Sweeney was already very familiar with a Stearman, having flown them from 1936 until 1957 and logging 2,000 hours aboard the plane. He first flew one himself at age 10 or 11, got a pilot's license before his driver's license and quickly became a crop duster in Mississippi and Illinois. Sweeney took his daughter Diane for rides as a child and she loved it. Other kids didn't like it so much, as Diane remembered, "He was merciless by doing loops when taking kids for a ride." Sweeney teared up slightly at this.

Sweeney smiled after his flight and said, "I wish I had a dollar for every time I have been up in one of these things. My last flight was in a club plane. This was wonderful!" As Sweeney looked back at the plane, daughter Diane said, "This was the perfect gift to him. He was like a kid going to Disney. We didn't tell him before we got here because we were afraid it would be too much for him. What a special day!"

Next on board was Don Stokes, an Army veteran who said he was famous for "putting Vic Damone in the infantry. Damone ended up with a tailored uniform and a Porsche." Damone was the famous singer, songwriter, and producer who Frank Sinatra said had the best "pipes" ever. Damone served from 1951-1953.

Stokes entered the Army in 1948 and was on leave out of Fort Lee, Virginia, when the Korean War broke out. Stokes said, "Everyone was called back to the base and sent overseas. Most of the guys from my barracks were killed, not much more than cannon fodder."

Stokes was sent to Heidelberg, Germany, for two years. At the time Berlin was divided among four countries, with about 3,000 Americans holding down their own quadrant. Stokes said, "Surprisingly, the subways were running and were the best way of transportation. Sometimes, men got off at the wrong country's stop and eventually had to be traded out. Most of what we did was top-secret. We were responsible for making sure that personnel were in the right place, in other words, the right number of riflemen and truck drivers where they were needed."

Stokes said the fighting in Korea seemed to come as a surprise to many veterans of WWII. "A lot of WWII guys went to the reserves and were then recalled for Korea and we almost had a mutiny because of it," he said.

Duty had a few humorous highlights too, according to Stokes. He said, "We took General Matthew Ridgeway's car and drove it around. People were saluting us because we were supposed to cover the name plate and didn't. Another time, my clothes were stolen and held for ransom. I was able to eventually get them back but was reassigned to a harder duty in order to get them."

Ray Smith, who served in the Navy from 1941-1945, signed up right out of college as a pilot cadet. Smith, at 97 years of age, recalled, "I had to do my own navigating and I wanted to fly fighters. I could never navigate by the stars, but I could make love under them. In 1942, I took a discharge from the Navy and went right into the Army Airborne. We flew Stearmans in both the Navy and Army and we called them the Yellow Peril. It was a nearly indestructible plane."

Smith, who's from Rhode Island, eventually became a glider pilot. He was stationed in England and then in southern France. Smith, called "Red" by those who know

him well, trained in the gliders for the upcoming invasion.
"The glider was like a silent chopper," he said. "My job was
to deliver 15 Black Berets behind the lines at Normandy.
About 90 percent of all gliders were made by a piano company. It was very sad over there because many of the gliders
didn't make it or couldn't land where they were supposed
to be. I landed mine where we planned to and once on the
ground, I went with the soldiers even though the pilots
were instructed to cross through the lines and return to
the beach." The gliders were "one and done," not to be used
again because there was no way get them back into the air.

When Smith's dream flight was delayed slightly, he told
Diane, "Take your time, fellows, I am over the hill anyway,
honey!" Smith moved to Florida in 1959 and became a
light-plane instructor. He was known for landing on Main
Street in Marco Island, just to have a few beers.

Director of Resident Relations Angela Proctor said, "Ray
loves to spend time at the dog track. He is in a hurry today
because he's got an appointment at the urologist."

Another Normandy veteran was Ray Drumm who served
in the Army for 27 months from 1943-45. Drum, 93, was
18 when he entered service during WWII and eventually
headed for the huge D-Day invasion by ship, before loading
on landing craft for the beach invasion. Drumm said, "We
were D-Day plus six days heading into Omaha Beach. We
lost a lot of men but we never got our feet wet. That landing
craft operator was good. We found a German crank phone

and tried to call Hitler just to tell him that we were coming and the Germans should go home. The Germans used wooden bullets in close combat. I carried an M1 rifle and two bandoliers into my first action."

Other actions included St. Lo where Drumm saw 3,000 bombers hit the town just ahead of his unit. The Battle of the Bulge had temperatures of 20 below zero. Drum said, "We were in a hole in the ground. Snow helped us keep warm because I only had one blanket."

Drumm was in Germany when the war ended. He said, "There was not a sound when we first heard. Everyone was in a daze. It was the best day of my life!"

Tank warfare was where Jack Whelan served in the Army from 1943 to 1946. Whelan and his M4 tank were not in Patton's Third Army but were trained by him. When serving at the Battle of the Bulge, Whelan said, "It snowed every night and there were no heaters. We did a 105-mile road march and I haven't been warm since. We dug a hole and pulled the tank over it. A tank crew had an engineer and included a loader and driver."

Known as the "Company Bootlegger," the 90-year-old Whelan added, "I could find booze anywhere. The sugar came from the Red Cross that helped us make our own booze. I am glad the Red Cross is still in business. Once, two of my guys got in a fight while making a booze trip in Russia. The company wanted to give one of them a Purple Heart for being wounded in action, but he wouldn't take it."

Whelan was originally interested in being a pilot but lost the chance when he was found to be color-blind. But he had good enough eyesight to serve on the bridge of the Queen Mary while looking for submarines when his unit was first sent overseas. They returned home through a hurricane, making for a rough journey.

An unusual memory showed that the danger was not over just because the Germans surrendered. Whelan said, "You couldn't walk down the streets of Berlin with a watch on. Someone would shoot you and take it. Once, we heard a jeep coming down the road and saw that it had a Russian major and his driver onboard. The major asked us how we liked his jeep, to which one of my guys showed him that the jeep was made in Dearborn, Michigan. The Russian major replied that the jeep was made in Russia instead.

Two Sport Clips volunteers, sisters Priscilla and Yvette Trevino, were mesmerized by these stories. Priscilla said, "I didn't know that these things had gone on. I loved listening to them tell about their service. This was the coolest thing that I have ever done."

Afternoon flying began with Norman Mytyk who served from 1967-69 during the Vietnam War. He served stateside and processed enlisted men both coming and going from Vietnam—"anybody from seventh-grade to PhDs," Mytyk said. "I often thought that those with the seventh-grade education made better conversation." Mytyk played both the piano and accordion.

Next for his dream flight was Lowell Hone, 85 years old, who also served stateside. Hone said, "I married right at the beginning of my service and the optometry degree made me a special recruit. I served in Missouri and took care of vision difficulties and helped with glasses. The government provided glasses and was good at it."

Hone served from 1953 to 1958, including helping with 18 German POWs after they were brought to the U.S. He later taught at Ohio State.

Army Private Buck Clyde's service was from 1942-1946, beginning in England once he went overseas. He went on to Germany by way of the Battle of the Bulge and the Remagen Bridge. Clyde said, "We were in the infantry. We ran and walked just about everywhere. I was most scared at the Battle of the Bulge where we had to fight our way out on two fronts. If you weren't scared, there was something wrong with you."

Once a captain asked Clyde if he was a driver, to which he replied, "I can drive but I don't have a military license. The captain told me that you do now." On another occasion, a German woman had a .38 pistol ready to shoot Clyde but for some reason didn't pull the trigger. "It took me a while to get over all of this," Clyde said. "I took my last drink the night after I got back home."

Burrington Terrace Engagement Director Christine Heaton, "The flyers this afternoon were all memory care patients and it was good to see them come out of their shell, especially Mr. Clyde. Words can't describe this. The flights are quite an experience, for them and for us. They certainly are the ones who deserve this attention."

The plane and the Winterboers moved on to Kissimmee for what they hoped was going to be a big Veteran's Day under beautiful blue skies. There was plenty of media attention scheduled for the morning with a local Fox morning show on site from 7:30 a.m. on.

With a DJ playing WWII period tunes in the background, Gene Reinhardt was the first flyer of the day. During the war, he was a Navy radioman on the Marshall Islands. The 90-year-old Reinhardt said, "When we heard that the war was over, we took a jeep and just drove around, not really believing that it was finally done. Then I later went back for Korea."

Admiring the Stearman, Reinhardt said, "This is a classic airplane for classic Americans!"

Up next was Thomas Utsey, who at 97 was the star of the day. As a young pilot, Utsey trained in a Stearman at Jackson, Mississippi. More training in a T-6 preceded deployment to North Africa where Utsey flew 55 missions as pilot of a B-25 bomber. Utsey said, "Completion of 50 missions was supposed to be enough that we could be sent back home, but they asked me to do 55. It all worked out and I got to come home before the war was over."

Utsey, who grew up in what he called the poorest section of Mississippi, spent 25 years flying for United Airlines, much of it in the early DC-3 planes. The AADF pilots often ask the dream flyers who were also pilots if they want to take the stick during flight, and Utsey was glad for the opportunity. Mike Winterboer said, "He was awesome in flying the plane and followed directions well." Upon stepping out of the plane, Utsey offered what was perhaps the quote of the week when he said, "I feel like a human being again!"

Rita Levreault, born in Massachusetts, was the last dream flyer for the day. She graduated in 1944 from Washington University and became a chemist for Monsanto. Later in life, Levreault returned to Amherst, Massachusetts, and became a teacher serving grades 5-12. She said, "I never listened when the students said they didn't like math. You just had to understand the students to guide them. Teaching was interesting but not hard." Levreault said she moved to Florida because she always enjoyed the weather there.

With this flight, Veteran's Day, 2016, came to a close for AADF.

CHAPTER 11

Voices from behind the scenes —
Mike Sommars, pilot

y wife, Lynn, and I have been married for over 38 years. Several years ago, with our three daughters all out of the house successfully pursuing their adult lives and with no grandchildren on the horizon, we began to discuss our lives ... and how lucky and blessed we have been. As an airline pilot, I still had many years until I would reach mandatory retirement at 65 years old and was quite happy seeing it through to the end. Lynn, on the other hand, was feeling stressed out and tired with her career as director of nursing at a skilled care retirement facility. Lynn has always been involved with the health industry since we first met. Psych tech (probably helped with raising me and our three daughters), LPN, RN, director of risk management, director of the ER and chief nursing officer were just some of the positions that she has held. All of those had been in a hospital setting, but for the past eight years or so, she had devoted her efforts to the senior, long-term care environment.

So it was with that background that we found ourselves having breakfast one morning in early 2014 at a local restaurant in Cave Creek, Arizona. For several months, we had been discussing a mutual desire to slow down, travel more, volunteer more and enjoy each other's company as we transition into retirement. While we were waiting for our order, another couple walked into the restaurant and sat nearby. We struck up a conversation with them and found out that they lived nearby, were only a few years older and recently retired. So naturally, we had to ask how they liked retirement and what they had found to occupy their time. They were excited to tell us how much they enjoyed retirement and how they filled their days ... designing greeting cards, knitting prayer shawls and picking up garbage alongside the roads. I looked at Lynn, whose eyes were glazing over and had a look on her face of "just shoot me now!" This was definitely NOT her idea of a transitioning into retirement.

Fast forward a couple of months and I'm in a pilot lounge at work in Phoenix visiting with Mike Winterboer. Mike and I had been acquaintances since the mid-1980s when we both worked as pilots at a small airport in Flagstaff, Arizona. We had both gone our separate ways until meeting again as new pilots at America West Airlines around 1990. At AWA, we never had the chance to fly together and since we lived in different parts of the country, we never had the chance to socialize. But we did always say hi and chat a bit when we saw each other. So as we visited that day, Mike told me that he had recently started flying a Stearman as a volunteer pilot with AADF. He had my interest at the word "Stearman" — a wonderful, iconic airplane that I was generously given an opportunity to fly almost 35 years earlier by its owner and rebuilder, a veteran of WWII and the Korean War. It was also the only airplane in which Lynn had genuinely enjoyed flying with me!

Mike and I continued to discuss what he was doing and I admitted it sounded like a lot of fun. He went on to say that he and his wife, Diane, were doing an AADF event in Oregon on a certain date in June and invited us to attend and see it firsthand. I made a note of the date but thought to myself, yeah … what's the chance of Lynn and I both having the time available for that? When I got home afterwards, Lynn and I discussed how much fun that would be … almost too good to be true. There had to be a catch!

Then, on just the slight chance we might have the time in our schedules to get to Oregon on those particular dates, we looked at the calendar. As part of our pre-retirement planning, we had "penciled-in" the northwest coast of Washington as an ideal place to retire, but felt that we should eliminate a few other places on our short list before committing. The first to be looked at was the Oregon coast … and on the date of Slim (Mike Winterboer) and Diane's AADF event, we already had vacation scheduled and a hotel reserved an hour's drive from the event! Lynn and I both felt upon that discovery that in the weighing of our retirement options, someone above our paygrade had their thumb on the scale! But still … there had to be a catch!

Lynn and I went on vacation and had a great time with the AADF event being the highlight and topic of our retirement discussions for the next several months. By October of that year, Lynn had resigned at her facility with a decision being made of starting her own long-term care consulting business. But not before insisting that the activities director make an application to have "Lynn's residents" be given the opportunity to be taken on a Dream Flight where we would have a chance to learn more about AADF.

Darryl called me before the event to introduce himself and ask if we would be able to attend, which for us was a given. We were there early and thoroughly enjoyed the response from "Lynn's residents." Lynn and I stayed late and took Darryl and his crew chief to dinner, trying to entice Darryl to reveal "the catch." No luck.

About a month later, Darryl called and said he needed a crew chief on short notice for a tour to move the Stearman from Yuma, Arizona, through California, over the Sierra Nevadas and ending in Dayton, Nevada. Lynn had just gone into surgery the previous day for scheduled hip replacement. As she was in otherwise great shape, recovering far ahead of schedule and we had relatives coming in to help with any errands, Lynn told me to have a great time … which I did! Once again, someone had their thumb on the scale for me to already have those days available.

It was on that trip that I met Augie, a genuine hero. Augie had lost his mom at a young age and was largely responsible for his younger brother and sister. He had gotten a job after school and on weekends at the airport sweeping out the hangar and doing general labor for a man that owned a couple of airplanes and gave flight instruction, which was how he paid Augie. Sometime just before WWII, Augie's dad decided to pack it in, soon leaving for Italy after telling Augie that he had to take care of the kids. Augie struggled for a while supporting his siblings anyway he could, while he avoided the law.

After a while, Augie decided that the best way to accomplish both goals (support his siblings and avoid the law) was to enlist. He tried to get into both the Navy and Army as a pilot, but at the time they both required a college degree. So instead, Augie joined the Marines and was trained as a machine-gunner. I believe it was at Guadalcanal that Augie's unit took massive casualties. After the airfield was captured, the Marines occupied it and based Dauntless Dive Bombers there.

The planes were short of qualified machine gunners and Augie volunteered. On one mission, his pilot was shot and both would have likely been killed were it not for Augie's actions. Although the controls in the rear machine-gunners' cockpit were very rudimentary, Augie was able to bring the aircraft back to base to land it. The Marines decided that a college degree was not necessary and put Augie in the pilot's seat of a Dauntless.

After a few missions as a pilot, Augie was shot down over water with his machine gunner badly injured. He was rescued after several days in the water but had been unable to save the machine gunner. After Augie recovered, he told his commanding officer that he didn't want to fly with another person onboard his airplane because he couldn't bear being responsible for another man's life again. His commanding officer agreed and soon had Augie training in the F4U Corsair, one of the greatest American aircraft of the war and greatly feared by the enemy.

After meeting Augie and Darryl giving him a flight during which Augie flew the aircraft (Darryl said he did great!), we ventured on to the next airport for an event with the residents of an assisted-living facility. The activities director was a hoot and her residents loved teasing her as much as she enjoyed teasing them. One veteran WWII pilot took me aside with his wife, with tears in his eyes, and thanked me for the opportunity AADF had given him to fly again.

From there, Darryl and I headed for Dayton via Lake Tahoe. Although it's pretty cold at 9,000 feet over Lake Tahoe in late October, I didn't really consider this to be "the catch" I was looking for. Just the opposite actually, with seeing the majestic beauty of mountains, forests and snow from a few hundred feet above. Of course, it wasn't until later that I realized that Darryl was just "setting the hook"!

In the two years since that introduction, Lynn and I have

traveled all over the country at 500 to 9,000 feet above the ground. We have met incredible people along the way like the heroes of our earlier generations and the unsung heroes … the wives of those far from home, taking care of their young families by themselves and those working in the factories that fed the war machine. It seems like everywhere we go, casual observers are first curious about our mission and then want to do anything they can to help and to honor those who contributed and sacrificed so much.

I will admit that I do have my favorite "profile." Everyone we take in the Stearman loves it and thanks us for the opportunity. But for those that are well-off financially and in good health, I'm not sure that those emotions last more than a few days, or even hours. Conversely, for those that are more frail, maybe feeling a sense of their own mortality while already having spent down their savings, it might just mean more. Maybe they are on Medicare or a small fixed income and have given up on ever doing something as adventuresome as a ride in an open cockpit bi-wing plane. For those, there are often emotional responses that can be overwhelming … for them and for us. While the former group will give genuine heartfelt thanks and then go on their way, the latter group will likely be more introspective of their past experiences and current state. They will linger, basking in just a fraction of the attention that they once had when they were leaders of their communities, and are now appreciative of having a meaningful conversation with someone outside of their community. Give me the guy in hospice care or the "little old lady" that with a wink of her eye might call me "Cheeky" or "might get kinda' fresh" any day!

As Lynn and I were counting down the hours of our last event, just as we have for every other last event, we were talking and trying to formulate and describe how we feel prior to an event. We decided that it feels like how we felt when we were kids and getting ready for Christmas. We never knew exactly what would be underneath the gift wrapping or what surprises we would be blessed with. We just always knew that we would enjoy the experience ... some more than others. That is just what we have learned to expect, anticipate and appreciate for an event. Every one of these people, from the ol' curmudgeon complaining about us being late to the gal planting a kiss on my cheek, they are all gems. They are unique in their own "story." Just like Forest Gump's box of chocolates, we never know what we are going to get.

In closing, I will propose that we have found the perfect opportunity to combine our two completely separate career paths into what we had sought earlier. We may not have slowed down any but we are traveling more, volunteering more and enjoying each other's company more! Oh, and we have found the catch, actually two of them. The first is that we have so much fun doing this that we have a tendency to over-commit, leaving little time to get anything else done. Days after finishing one tour and thinking we need to back away from it for a while, we are looking at our schedules to see when we can work in another tour! The second is that it is more expensive than we first thought, due to our new-found love of small airplanes and flying to remote areas. We recently purchased our own aircraft, not a Stearman because I already have the keys to three of these. This is a Cessna Skywagon, an aircraft typically used as a bush plane in Alaska. We're still planning our retirement and thinking a gig flying tourists in Alaska beats picking up garbage along the roads any time!

LYNN SOMMARS
Crew chief, social media, training

Wow, how do I summarize?

How do I describe Bunny from Nebraska? Waiting in the van wrapped in a blanket in his wheelchair, a shell of a man. Bunny was in hospice care and his family causally stated to Diane in scheduling, "It's OK if he dies while up there." As a nurse, I had huge reservations about this. It was a very cold day and as I entered the van to talk to the man (who had cheek bones and eyes as the most prominent parts of his face), he was wrapped from head to toe in blankets to keep warm. I asked him, "Do you want to do this?" and he looked sincerely at me and nodded his head. He had no strength and probably weighed 80 pounds. The caregiver at his side said, "I've got this," and lifted him easily and with the help of my husband, Mike, and a Sport Clips volunteer,

Bunny was soon in the plane. We wrapped him up and off he went. Bunny passed away a few days later.

How do I capture for you the war bride that flew with her husband's love letters that he, as a pilot, had written to her during the WWII era? She was so emotional that she struggled to speak and had to be taken back to the retirement community immediately after the flight. Several weeks later we received a beautiful letter from her telling us that she "heard her husband's voice as she re-read the letters in her mind."

Or the non-flying resident in Colorado whose son brought him to watch the event? The son was a bit angered that the community where his dad resided had not invited him to come. This beautiful white-haired man, wheelchair bound with very swollen feet and ankles, urine running into a bag, spent the entire day with his son reliving his days in the military. We brought both of them out to the plane, his son proudly relaying to Mike the victories his dad had. Mike truly enjoyed hearing his stories and listened intently. Mike thanked the man for his service, placed a signed hat on his head and closed the conversation with a solid handshake. When our friend passed away a few months later, we received a letter from his son that this was the biggest highlight his dad had experienced in years and AADF was listed as a beneficiary of his will. Both Mike and I became teary as we shook our heads in unison regarding this huge honor. We were humbled.

I spent the first 20-some years as a nurse in a fast-paced environment and learned that getting too close to any patient would not do well in this profession. In the emergency room, we said good-bye to many, leaving grieving families to fend for themselves and to go home alone.

Out of the blue came an offer to lead a team of professionals to provide dignity and care to the elderly and I accepted without any further thought. My heart told me I had made the right decision. The exposure to long-term care brought new breath to a tired nurse, yet that job itself became so overwhelming that I knew I had to make another change.

The morning after I resigned, I stood outside on my patio without a job or vision of what I was going to do. I was 55 and had worked since I was 14. Our three daughters were living happy and successful lives. I had nothing on the horizon and felt empty with no idea of what to do. A calm voice said to me, "I have something great in store for you!" I knew everything would be OK. I felt peace. I felt good.

That same good feeling came to me while I visited the "Rosie Riveters" at our first contact with AADF. Mike and Diane Winterboer were bringing out huge genuine smiles that — as I knew from experience working with folks in care centers and assisted livings — don't come out very often.

My husband and I looked at each other and we knew that this was it. THIS was exactly what we needed, yet we had no idea how it would blend our professional careers together. Already we had grown a deep respect for each other's knowledge.

I could go on and on. I haven't mentioned the Alzheimer's resident who trained in the Stearman and taught students for years as career military. He hadn't spoken in almost a year and I had huge reservations letting him go up in the plane, but Mike didn't. When they landed, he got out of the plane and took Mike's hands and stated, "You took me to a place in heaven that I haven't been to in years." I still get teary eyed when I tell that story.

We flew another man recently in California who spoke normally until he opened up about the pain and all the guilt he has carried all these years. He stated in a stuttering voice, "I need to go to heaven so I can say I am sorry to all of those beautiful young Japanese boys that I had killed." He was a scout that gave the go ahead to begin shooting.

I love the WASPS and can I have an entire chapter about them?

For two people that have been married for almost 38 years and were searching for a new chapter, we have found ourselves surrounded by an entire book of memories. We laugh, we cry and we work harder than we thought possible. When we collapse after a 14-hour day, we say, "I never have been this tired and I have never been so happy!"

We get to take those who fly and often their families back to a place where they used to be. Mike and I get a glimpse of who they were just for a short time. We get to experience it with them! We both plan to contribute to AADF as long as we are physically able to perform our duties as I can't imagine not hearing more ......

Thanks for allowing me to share a bit of our two blessed years with Ageless Aviation Dreams Foundation.

CAROL FISHER
Controller

Darryl and his father, Bill, flew commercially to Mississippi to pick up Bill's bi-plane which had been restored, and on the way back they had given rides at three or four assisted living centers on the way to Oregon. After Darryl returned from Mississippi with the plane, he mentioned that people had wanted to give them money. Darryl wasn't doing it for the money so he refused their offer. I suggested that we form a 501(c)(3) charitable organization so that when people wanted to donate, then they could get a tax write-off. It was then decided that we would only operate on donated funds and when the funds ran out, the rides would stop.

In Dayton, Nevada, I am the controller of mission senior living, the management company for our assisted living centers. I have been a legal assistant, a real estate agent and an accountant. I went back to college to become an attorney after an AA degree in Legal Secretary and working for attorneys. I met Darryl in Spanish class when finishing my B.A. I also received my Mrs. that same year of 1988. I like cooking tasty vegetarian food, gardening, snow skiing and hiking. I do the accounting and legal work for AADF.

The skills that I have made it possible to get the foundation started and continue to grow as the foundation grows. I have always been Darryl's supporter in whatever adventures come our way. Although I have only participated in local events and the 1,000th flight in Minnesota, I enjoy visiting with the veterans and never cease to be amazed at the bravery and skill these men and women possess that only a few around them may completely appreciate.

CHAPTER 12

More voices from behind the scenes —
Merilyn Chaffee, vice president and scheduling

I met Darryl through a mutual friend, Tom Smith, at the Santa Rosa airport. Tom and I attended the same church and shared a mutual love of flying. His wife, Debbie, and I share a love of music, and our two families became close friends during the seven years that my husband was pastoring at the Santa Rosa SDA Church. I worked as a flight instructor at the Santa Rosa airport part-time. Tom said to me one day, "I have a friend who flies a Stearman and you should come out to the airport to meet him!"

Always up for an adventure, especially if it involves airplanes, I was all for it. Tom had arranged for me to fly an Albatross and land it in Lake Berryessa a few months before, so I knew that if Tom asked whether I wanted to go to the airport, the answer was an unequivocal yes! I was especially interested in this particular airplane because in high school my dad, being a wise father of four teenagers, bought a Kitfox experimental plane and told my siblings that when it was put together, he would teach us to fly.

The box showed up with a million pieces and had a three ring binder of directions. The garage became our aircraft shop. We spent every afternoon and weekend putting the plane together. In the meantime, my pilot father got my oldest brother his flight instructor certificate. A year and a half later, the plane was done, and my brother taught me to fly in it when I was 17. Now, with well over 1,000 hours on the Kitfox, I am now teaching my 17-year-old nephew to fly it in a full circle moment.

Back to the Stearman in Santa Rosa. The Kitfox is a high-wing taildragger and has some similar flying characteristics to the Stearman and this made it most interesting to meet Darryl and fly the really cool old war bird. I arrived at the airport just after the last veteran had left, but enjoyed meeting Darryl. He graciously took me up for a flight, which I felt was especially nice as he had already given about a dozen veteran rides that day. As we taxied out and took off flying north of the little town of Healdsburg, Darryl gave me the controls and I was instantly in love with the plane. It's such a thrill to experience the wind in your face, the control stick that is so responsive to minute input, the substantial and stable feel of the plane and round roar of the engine coupled with the feeling of connection to those who learned to fly in this plane and went on to fight for my freedom.

I wasn't expecting the emotional response I had as we soared over the vineyards and low hills of Northern California. It was terrain that I flew over daily, but being in the Stearman somehow made me see it with new eyes. After the flight, Tom and Debbie, along with their pilot daughter Katie, invited Darryl and me to dinner. All I can remember about the meal was laughing until I had tears streaming down my face from the stories. Tom and Darryl told of their early years flying around in the hopper of Darryl's uncle's crop-dusting Stearman, Tom puking from the fumes left in it and Darryl pitching Tom out at some random place in Oregon for his parents to come collect. I wondered how the two of them, both giants, could even get the Cessna off the ground. They told of flying to a random snow field and not being sure they would ever get back out and the hijinks they pulled getting it back in the air. The stories and laughter continued as the evening progressed and Darryl shared about AADF. I remember saying, "If you ever need help with your foundation, let me know! This is the kind of thing that I could really get behind."

My family lives on a mandarin farm in Paradise, California. My husband is a pastor at our local church and we have three children, Lilliana (12), Makayla (10) and Grayson (9). I grew up flying with my dad, a thoracic surgeon in a very rural area of Northern California. He would fly on Tuesdays to his post-op patients to avoid them having to make two-to-four-hour drives along winding roads to come back to the hospital for a ten-minute check of incisions, blood pressure, etc. He would take one of his kids on each flight.

He would let us sit on pillows so we could peer over the dash and we would feel like big stuff as we gripped the control wheel of his Piper Saratoga. We anxiously glanced back and forth between the altimeter and attitude indicator to make sure that we were keeping things straight and level. I remember falling in love with flying on these trips and will forever be grateful to my father for sharing his love of serving people and flying with me.

As a teenager, I got my license and went on to get my instrument and commercial ratings in high school. In college, I decided I wanted to fly missionary flights, eventually contacting the Missionary Aviation Fellowship asking if they would send me somewhere to serve as a student missionary for a year. They told me that flying the plane was only about half of what I would need in the mission field and that I had to get my Airframe and Powerplant Technician's license before they would consider me. So I went to Andrews University to get said A&P rating. While there, I figured out that in the time that it would take me to complete the FAA prescribed hours in the shop, I could get my Certified Flight Instructor's ticket and graduate with a Bachelor's of Technology in Aviation. That is what I did.

While in Michigan, I felt like teaching might be what I was meant to do. After graduating, I came back to California and taught flying while getting a master's degree in education. Over the past 30 years, I have met and married a pastor, had three children who bring joy to my life and light to my days. I have flown lots of fun planes and taught lots of amazing people to fly, taught many children in the classroom and a few teachers at the collegiate level. Now I enjoy being involved with AADF, which combines my love of flying and love of service and is a wonderful part of my life.

I flew a tour in California with Mike and Lynn, and then Darryl. Meeting the veterans face to face, hearing their stories and seeing the tears and joy after flying again, hearing from family members after the fact who are so very thrilled makes my day. They talk about how life changing and life bringing the flight was, and their joy has become part of the wonderful experiences I have had with AADF in the year of involvement. Honestly, who else has a job where everyone they call to talk to is thrilled to hear from you? The facility directors love this opportunity for their residents, the independent flyers are beyond excited about getting to fly again (and for free!), the family members are so excited to hear about it, the airports are happy to be a part of something good, especially once they know us and what we stand for. The PR doesn't hurt either. It is a real joy to be part of AADF!

While on the tour, one old timer came over and took my arm and said, "You know, the pilot, he's all right. But you, you're the crew chief! You are the one with the power, and he's nothing. He can only taxi when you tell him to. He can only go where you tell him to. So you just let him know that if he gets out of line. Or I can set him straight for you!" I enjoyed telling my boss when he taxied back for the next flyer that he was nothing and I would be the one to let him know when and where from here on out.

I would love to fly tours with my husband sometime in the future when our kids are a little older. He has all the people skills and the veterans would love him. I love to fly and think the women pilots especially would love to fly with me. For now, I coordinate the scheduling and am enjoying this part of my journey, but I'm looking forward to getting into the cockpit when it won't be so obvious to my kids that I am gone for four or five days at a time.

WENDY D'ALESSANDRO
Publicity and marketing

I met Diane Winterboer while doing media outreach for the Dream Flights for one of our client's retirement communities. Each time I hung up the phone with Diane, I was smiling. I loved hearing the stories about the Dream Flights and the veterans and their families. I found it unbelievable that a group of people would volunteer their own personal time to travel the country and bring such joy to a most deserving group of people. And then there were the bi-planes — those colorful, historic aircraft just added to what I already thought was such a great story. I love a good story and with every Dream Flight event, there are at least six or seven new stories for me to hear or read about.

At the time, I had just started my own PR firm. I believe in giving back and I wanted to incorporate that philosophy into my business by bringing on one organization as a pro-bono account. The organization had to reflect or offer something that I truly believed in and I had to believe that my efforts would help contribute to its success. Also, I wanted to have some fun while I worked the account. If you don't love what you do, you won't do it very well. So when choosing that pro-bono account, I have to believe in the organization and there needs to be synergy with the people I work with. Life's too short to surround yourself with work and people who don't inspire you.

Diane connected me with Darryl and I offered to provide media outreach support of AADF. Honestly, I think I approached my conversation with Darryl with a sales pitch-like tone. I wanted AADF as a pro-bono account and was hoping they would want me to join their team. The whole crew has been gracious and appreciative of our efforts. I love working this account and wish I could afford to do more for them.

Lynn PR provides PR services for Covenant Retirement Communities, which has 15 retirement communities in 10 states. As you can imagine, we've had many opportunities to welcome Darryl and his crew. More than 100 of our residents have been honored with Dream Flights. The first was in Chicagoland, at Covenant Village of Northbrook. Pitching this story to the Chicagoland media was so much fun. From that point on, every time I learned one of our client's communities was scheduled for a Dream Flight, I was beaming.

I wish I could pinpoint what draws me to AADF. It makes no sense, really, since I can't fly a plane, have no military background, can't schedule a flight and still must Google to make sure I am getting my historical and military facts straight. Technically, I'm not qualified to be part of this crew. But yet, I am inspired by this group and believe in what they are doing. These are good people, exceptional people when you get to know them, sharing their talent and time to honor a generation of heroes while expecting nothing in return.

Perhaps it's the story. I love a good story and this one is pure, through and through. Magical even, because Darryl and his crew have been able to rally a group of like-minded individuals with a passion for flying, a passion for seniors and a passion for honoring military veterans. This organization could never sustain itself without a true commitment from everyone involved.

I could talk with the veterans for hours. I was hooked on the stories and there have been many times that I have sat in front of my computer wiping away a few tears. Our veterans are incredibly special and it makes me happy to be part of an organization that is making a difference in their lives. It's the same reason I am drawn to the senior living industry. That is my job, yes, but my efforts are helping others enhance the lives of older adults and their families. That means something to me.

I remember talking with Darryl's dad, Bill, for a few hours concerning an article we were writing about AADF. I could hear the pride in his voice when he talks about his son's path in life and I could hear that same pride in Darryl's voice when he talks about his dad. The Fisher family seems to have a calling to serve, in some form, either through government, senior living or AADF. That says something about their character and their purpose.

Every Dream Flight is a new story and I never tire of hearing a new story. My dad and grandfathers served in the military but no one ever spoke of their experiences. I don't think I fully appreciated the men and women who served until I listened to the stories firsthand or read their stories from Diane and Merilyn's detailed notes. Our military veterans and their families deserve to be recognized, thanked and honored. Supporting AADF is one way I can quietly show my appreciation.

One might think that my best experience so far would be my first Dream Flight. The flight was amazing, breathtaking and one of my best experiences ever. I have a photo of me wearing a canvas helmet and grinning ear-to-ear tacked on my office bulletin board. I had expected to feel a lot of wind and chaos, but instead the flight felt incredibly peaceful and still.

It was during this Dream Flight event in Florida (I've

only participated in two Dream Flight events) that I experienced the magic that everyone talks about. Talking with the Dream Flight recipients and their families, seeing the smiles, watching one gentleman's grayish blue eyes look so soulful and raw after his flight, yet he was beaming with a smile, that is when you know that the program is special.

It was here that I watched Diane Winterboer talking with a woman who was scheduled to fly. You could see Diane's sincerity and affection and you could see from the veteran's expression that she was making a connection. I watched her that day talk to every single person with the same focus and individualized attention. She already knew something of their stories but wanted to know more. Diane listened and they knew that she was listening and I believe that matters to this population.

When the crew talks about the magic, it's not just the magic created by the flight itself. The magic starts when the veterans learned they are being honored with the Dream Flights. It's the preparation and the anticipation of the day's events. It's being whisked away to the local airport and breathing in that fresh air while they wait their turn. It's the mayor's speech, the color guard and the media frenzy. It's the one-on-one attention and the freedom to share their stories with people who care and want to know more. The Dream Flight itself is a magical highlight to an extraordinary day.

DIANE WINTERBOER

Mike and I were together at an air show in Hillsboro, Oregon, in July of 2013 when we met Darryl and learned about the Foundation. Mike offered to help fly and took lessons in the Stearman from Preston Aviation in Florida the following spring. Mike started flying with Darryl in April, 2014. I offered to help schedule for the Foundation and did so for 2014 and 2015 along with being Mike's ground crew.

We live in Oregon and Mike is a commercial pilot. His aviation experience has given him the skillset to fly the Stearman. He also has an interest in the World War II generation. I am a wildlife biologist by trade and coordinated and organized a statewide program as a liaison between a federal and state agency among other things. We both love history and travel and feel like this is a ministry during which we can love on others.

Our first experience with the Foundation was in Decatur, Illinois, in September of 2013. We were there visiting family when we found out that Darryl would be arriving to fly a WWII friend of my sisters. Bob Falstrom told Darryl he didn't feel like he did much during his military years since he only worked in the Pentagon. Darryl's response was, "You would have done whatever they asked you to, wouldn't you have?" Bob responded that he would have, and Darryl assured him that he was well beyond worthy of a flight. Mike helped Darryl load Bob into the plane and we saw the impact that the flight had on him. Bob's adult daughter came out to watch and we could see that his Dream Flight created a special moment between the two of them. It was an emotional experience and it hooked us!

We have had more "best experiences" than we can list. Picking one would be as impossible as listing them all. We can only sum them up by listing what we love most about doing this. It's about loading a 90-year-old into the plane and getting a 19-year-old out, seeing the families witness their loved one do what they thought was now physically impossible. We saw an older veteran dance gleefully with his adult daughter when she had not seen him have such joy since losing his wife months ago. Many of their stories were never taught in our history classes. We love meeting activity directors that go above and beyond to make the event day extra special for everyone. Traveling together and seeing this amazing country from a different perspective is wonderful.

I have been surprised at how the veterans will tell me stories they haven't shared with their own families. I didn't see this coming at all and it is very humbling. I have learned that a 90-year-old is just a 20-year-old in disguise. They have an amazing sense of humor, they love to laugh and they love to be heard and respected. Another thing I enjoy is when we ferry the plane from one location to the next. It sure can get cold in the plane and I was surprised that someone makes battery-powered socks.

The events are often exhausting physically and emotionally. There are days when I cry along with the veterans and I'm zapped at the end of the day.

The Foundation has changed us personally and also changed our marriage. We have gained a new appreciation for the men and women who served our country. I have always heard that veterans made sacrifices but I didn't fully understand what they meant. I am more patriotic now. Mike and I work better as a team because of our Foundation experience. On the road, we rely on each other so much to make the trips and events run smoother.

Mike and I are both in awe of the blessings upon this Foundation. We have seen only a few cancellations despite the age of the planes, weather limitations and countless other factors that could have shut us down. The right people at the right time always are there to help. We always seem to have what we need when we need it, like a van with a removable center console to haul a replacement propeller. All of this has also strengthened our faith.

WASP Mary Helen Foster in Spring, TX.

Eugene Bell, U.S. Marines, with son, Tim, in Spring, TX.

Leslie Marshall with Kacey from Sport Clips in Friendswood, TX.

Barbra Kiward with Nancy Orozco from Sport Clips in Spring, TX.

Ted Simkus, U.S. Army, in Atlanta, GA.

Bill Kirkpatrick, U.S. Navy, in Atlanta, GA.

Jeffrey Heal, Vietnam veteran, in Atlanta, GA.

Helen Chapman, WAC, in Atlanta, GA.

Doris and Fred Hatterick, U.S. Navy, in Atlanta, GA.

John Gass, U.S. Marines, in Atlanta, GA.

Annie Veal, U.S. Air Force, in Atlanta, GA.

Morris Berg, U.S. Marines, in Atlanta, GA.

James Armstrong, U.S. Air Force, in Atlanta, GA.

Herman
and
Margaret
Snelling,
U.S. Army,
with
Salisbury,
N.C., Mayor
Karen
Alexander,
Salisbury,
N.C.

Bob Horand,
U.S. Army,
in Salisbury,
N.C.

Tom Nolan
U.S. Marines,
in Salisbury,
N.C.

Earl Graves
U.S. Navy,
in Salisbury,
N.C.

Walter Leather
U.S. Navy,
in Salisbury,
N.C.

Ron Hands,
U.S. Army,
in Salisbury,
N.C.

Ned Thomas,
U.S. Air Force,
in Salisbury,
N.C.

Clarence Guenther in Waukesha, WI.

Robert Muehlbauer, U.S. Marines, in Milwaukee, WI.

Ed Aufderheide, U.S. Marines, in Waukesha, WI.

Jack Whitefield, U.S. Navy, in Waukesha, WI.

Bob Nieman in Waukesha, WI.

Bob Loss with daughter in Waukesha, WI.

Rosemary Anderson, cadet nurse, in Northbrook, IL.

Tom Blim, U.S. Navy, with daughter in Northbrook, IL.

Eddie Lamken, U.S. Army, in Stevens Point, WI.

Tom Bredow, U.S. Navy, in Stevens Point, WI.

George Nugent, U.S. Navy, with family in Stevens Point, WI.

WWII veteran Terry Menze, U.S. Navy, in Stevens Point.

Karl Pierson, U.S. Army, in Batavia, IL, with Tim Newton, AADF pilot.

Dom Errichiello, U.S. Army, in Carol Stream, IL.

Emmitt Gaffron, U.S. Army, in Decatur, IL.

Jim Hord, U.S. Army, in Decatur, IL.

Ivan Wiley, U.S. Army, in Decatur, IL.

Brunhilde Fischer in Decatur, IL.

Jack Sutherland with Tyfanni Allen from Sport Clips, in Decatur, IL.

Lloyd Smith, U.S. Army, in Oxford, MS. This was the 2,000th Dream Flight.

Earnest Aune, U.S. Air Force, pictured with his sons in Oxford, MS.

Angus Emerson, U.S. Army, in Oxford, MS.

Hugh Newton, first Dream Flight, in Oxford, MS.

Bob Campbell, 1,000th Dream Flight, pictured with Darryl Fisher.

Steve Toma in Oxford, MS.

Darryl
flying the
T-38.

Edward Kissam, Merchant Marine, in Jacksonville, FL.

Ernie Sweeney, U.S. Army, in Ft. Myers.

Ray Smith, U.S. Army, in Ft. Myers, FL.

Ray Drumm, U.S. Army, in Ft. Myers, FL.

Jack Whelan, U.S. Army, in Ft. Myers, FL.

Thomas Utsey, U.S. Army Air Corp, Kissimmee, FL.

Buck Clyde, U.S. Army, in Ft. Myers, FL.

Mike Sommars, left, with Bunny.

Mike and Lynn Sommars

Charley Norton with Merilyn Chaffee in Tracy, CA.

Wendy
D'Alessandro

Mike and Diane Winterboer

AADF group picture in 2017

Milwaukee celebration

Stevens Point celebration

This Stearman (tail number 49295) was built in 1940 and was manufactured in the Boeing Airplane Company in Wichita, KS. It was used by the Army and stationed in Sikeston, MO, Hemet, CA, Oxnard, CA, Glendale, AZ and Ontario, Canada. A wholesaler located at the old Beaverton, OR., Airport bought it from the military after they turned it over to a disposal agency designated by the Surplus Property Board of the U.S. Government in 1945. William L. Fisher (founder's, Darryl, grandfather) purchased the plane in 1946 for $1,500 (the original cost of the airplane was approximately $11,000 in 1940). Bill Fisher, Darryl's father, took his first Stearman flight in this very aircraft. William sold it in 1948 to Wen Airco in Wenatchee, WA. In 1983, Tom Fisher (Darryl's uncle) purchased the plane to use as a spray plane. Darryl purchased the plane in 2004 and had it completely restored. This plane has flown four generations of the Fisher family and is near and dear to the family. It gave its first Dream Flight in July 2011. Today, it produces most of the Foundation's Dream Flights as it serves the eastern United States.

This Stearman (tail number 371SD) was built in 1942. It was also manufactured by Boeing in Wichita, KS, for approximately $9,000. Although the plane was commissioned by the Army, it was loaned to the Navy and sent to Naval Air Stations in New Orleans, LA; Lambert Field (St. Louis), MO; Dallas, TX; and Clinton, OK. It was turned over to the government surplus company in 1945 to be sold to private individuals. This aircraft was also used as a spray plane and later purchased by Bill Fisher then later, Darryl Fisher. It was fully restored around 2009. It gave its first Dream Flight in August of 2011. Now, it primarily serves the western United States.

This Stearman (tail number 58986) was built in 1944. Like the others, this was manufactured for the Army by the Boeing company in Wichita, KS, for approximately $9,000. It was stationed at Sequoia Field, CA (between Vilisa & Dinuba); Tulare, CA; Lancaster, CA; Bakersfield, CA; Sacramento, CA; and Ogden, UT. It was turned over to a government disposal company in 1950. It, too, was used as a spray plane and used by a family-owned business called Meek Dusters in California. Bill Fisher purchased it in 1982. Once the plane was restored, it gave the Foundation's very first Dream Flight on March 29, 2011 in Oxford, MS. This aircraft serves the midwest section of the U.S.

ABOUT THE AUTHOR

David Freeze loves a good adventure, especially if it involves travel and meeting people from across America. When Darryl Fisher proposed the concept of chronicling a  year in the life of Ageless Aviation Dreams Foundation, David was all for it. Young Again is the author's fifth book, combining travel and interesting Americans who this time just happened to be military veterans. Much of the travel came in the historic Stearman biplanes providing yet another unique view of our great country.

David is also a motivational speaker, emphasizing that regular people can achieve amazing things. Contact him at david.freeze@ctc.net. Walnut Creek Farm Publishing is named after his farm.

An accomplished runner and endurance cyclist, David's other four books cover various adventures across America by bicycle. He has completed over 80,000 running miles and 13,000 endurance cycling miles.

Other books by David Freeze include:
- **Lord, Ride with Me Today**
  The story of a solo coast-to-coast bicycle journey — 2013
- **Pedaling, Prayers and Perseverance**
  35 Days Cycling Solo from Maine to Key West — 2014
- **Riding the Rails to Freedom**
  Cycling the Underground Railroad Route from Alabama to Ontario — 2015
- **Highway to History**
  A Cycling Adventure on Route 66 — 2016

CPSIA information can be obtained
at www.ICGtesting.com
Printed in the USA
FSOW01n0620250517
34420FS